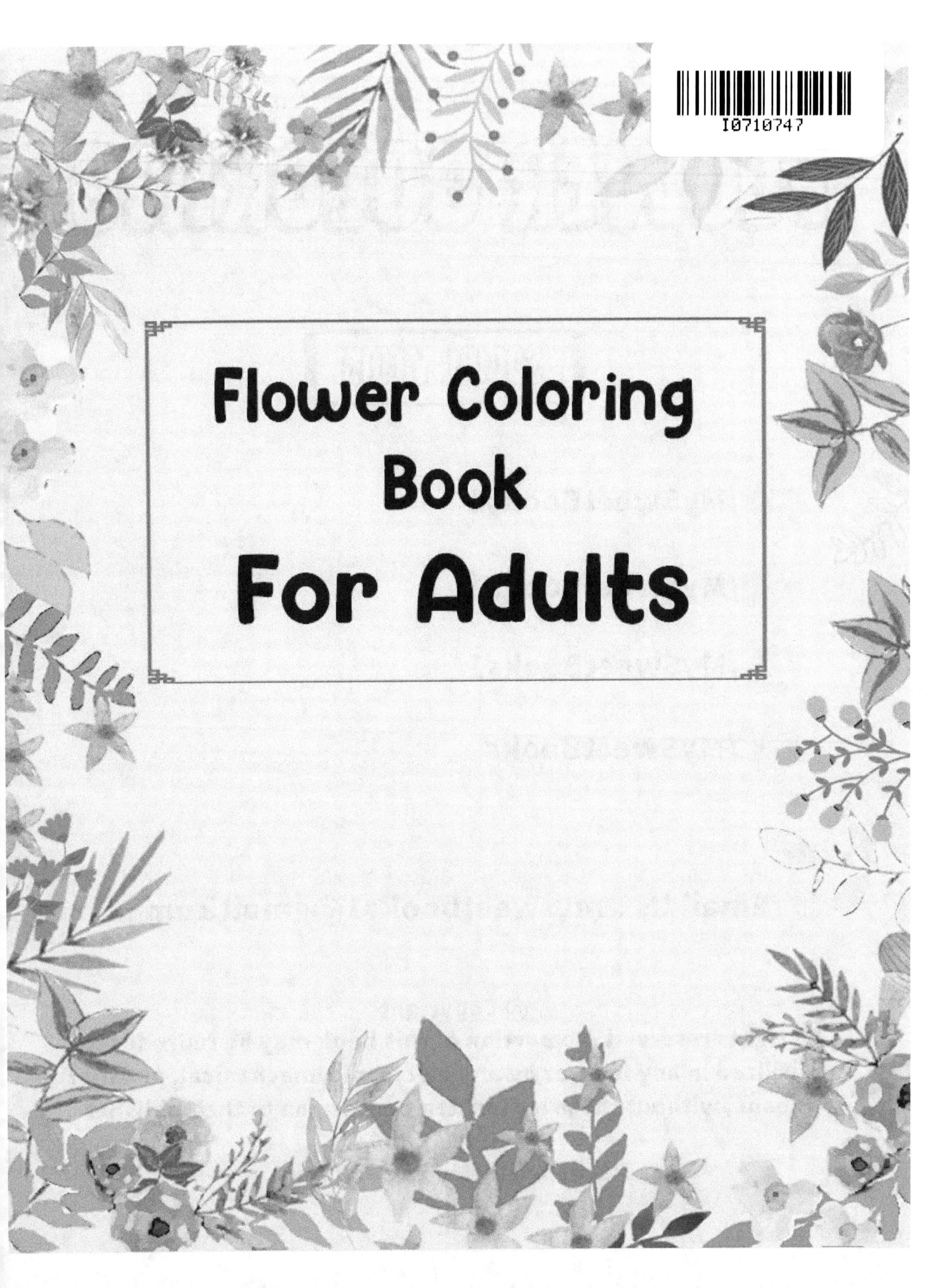

Flower Coloring Book
For Adults

FLOWER COLORING

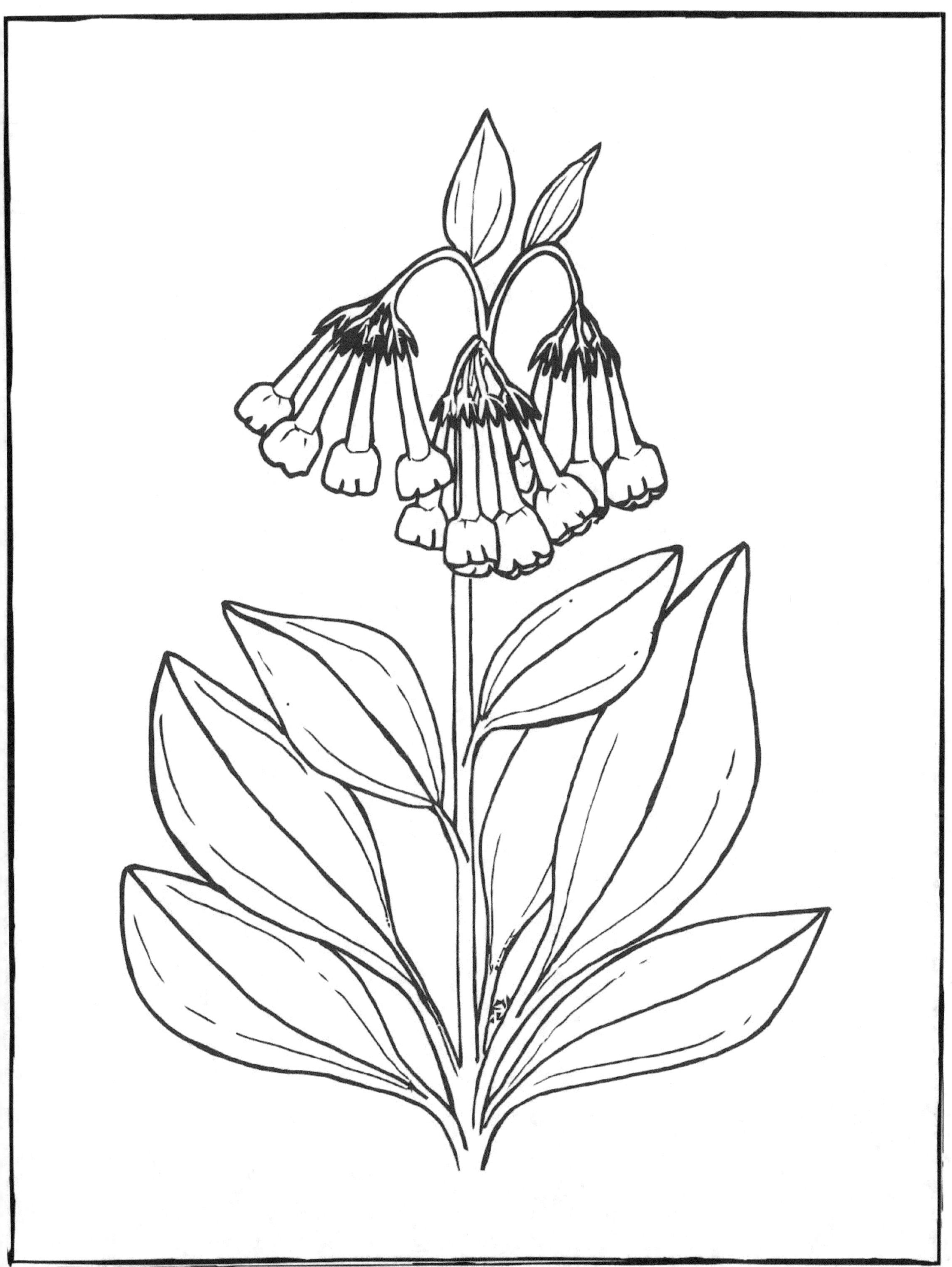

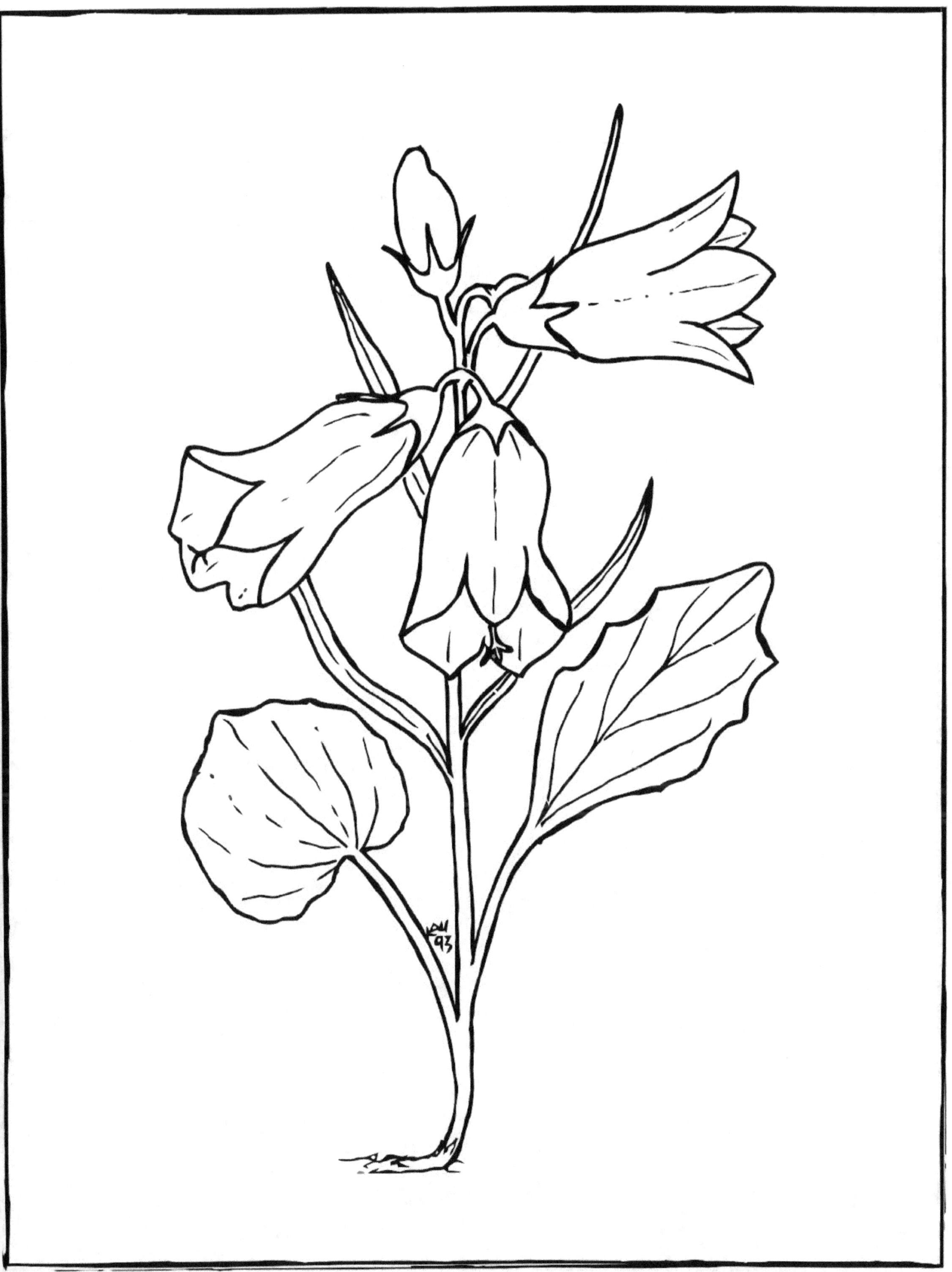

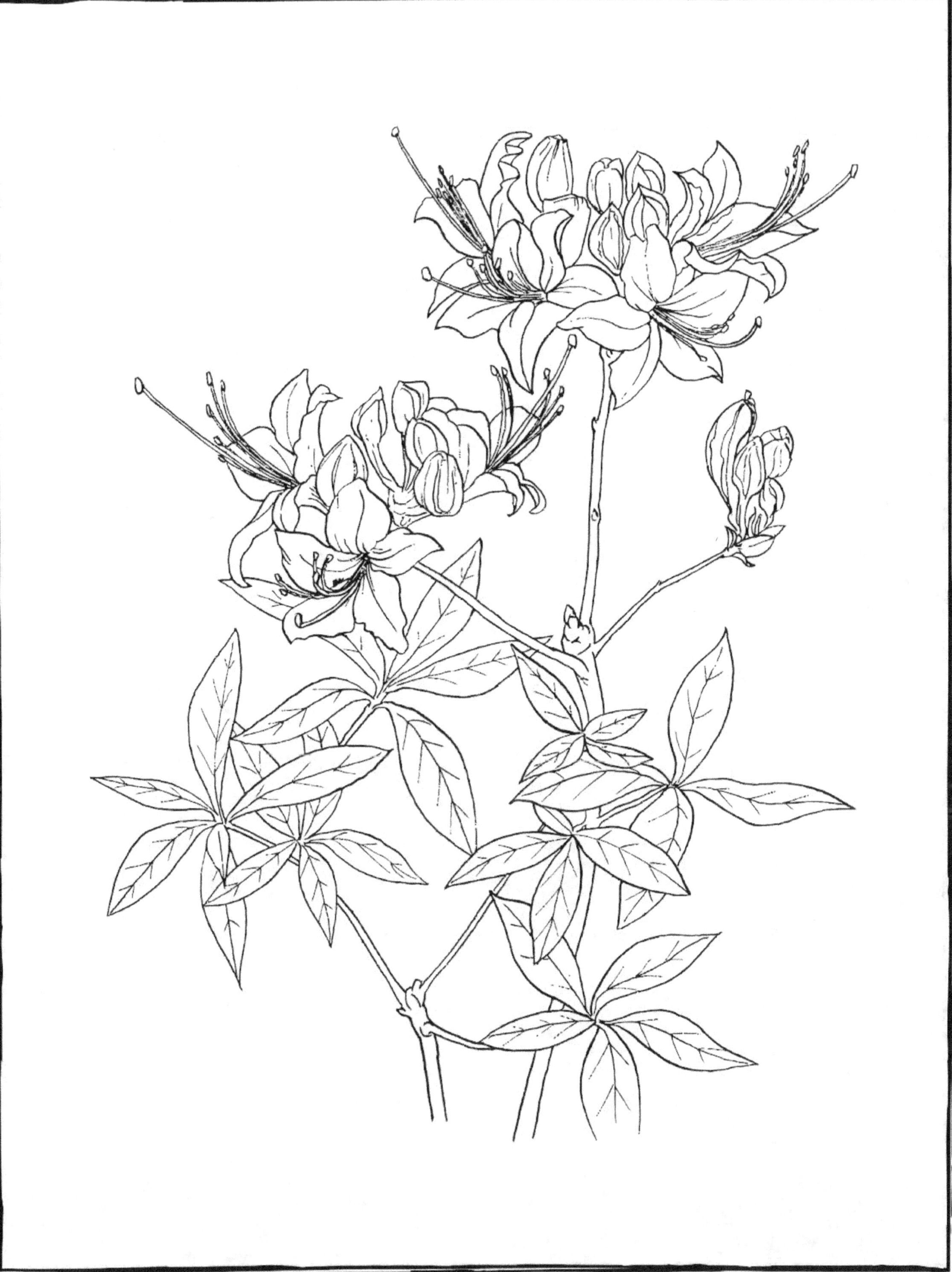

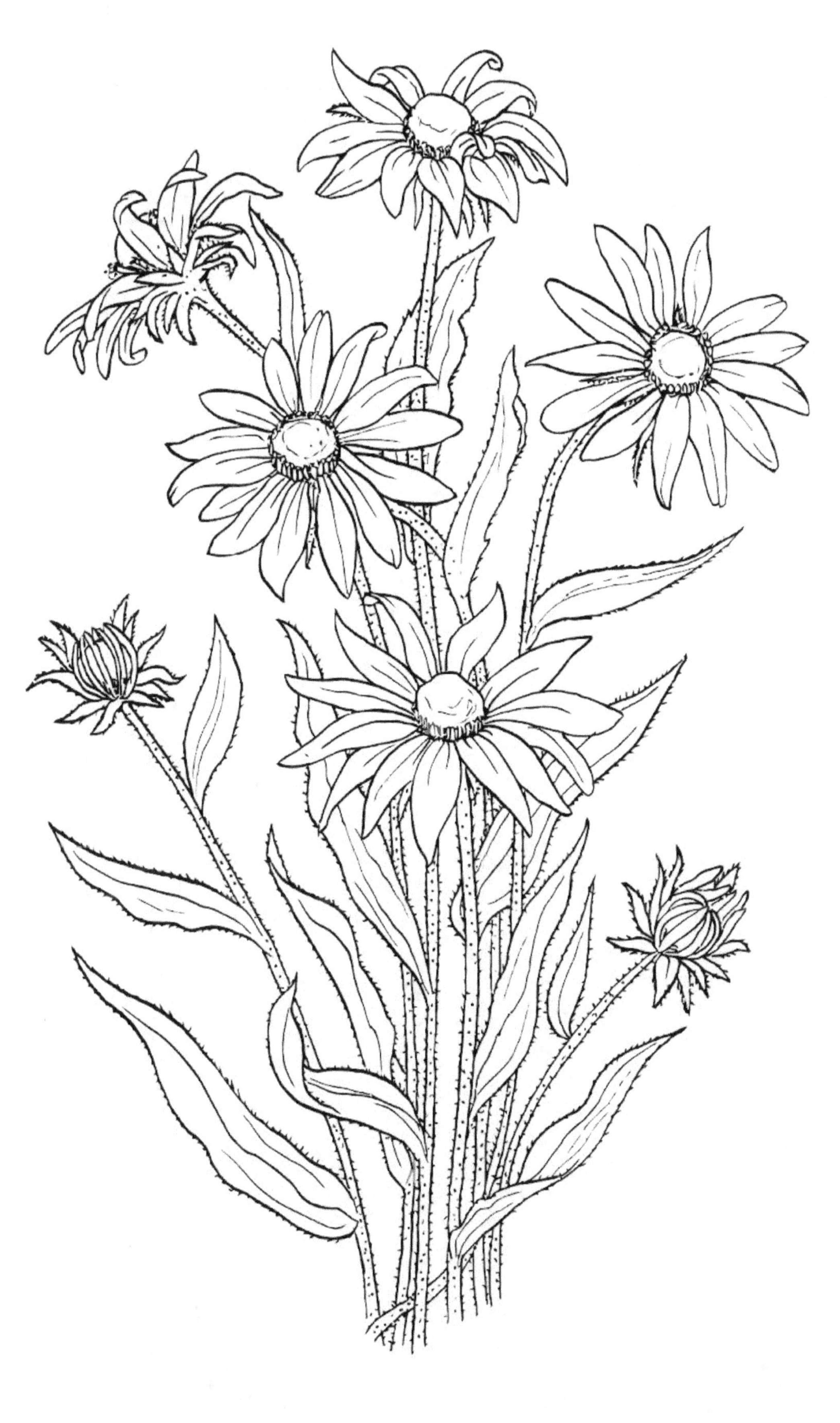

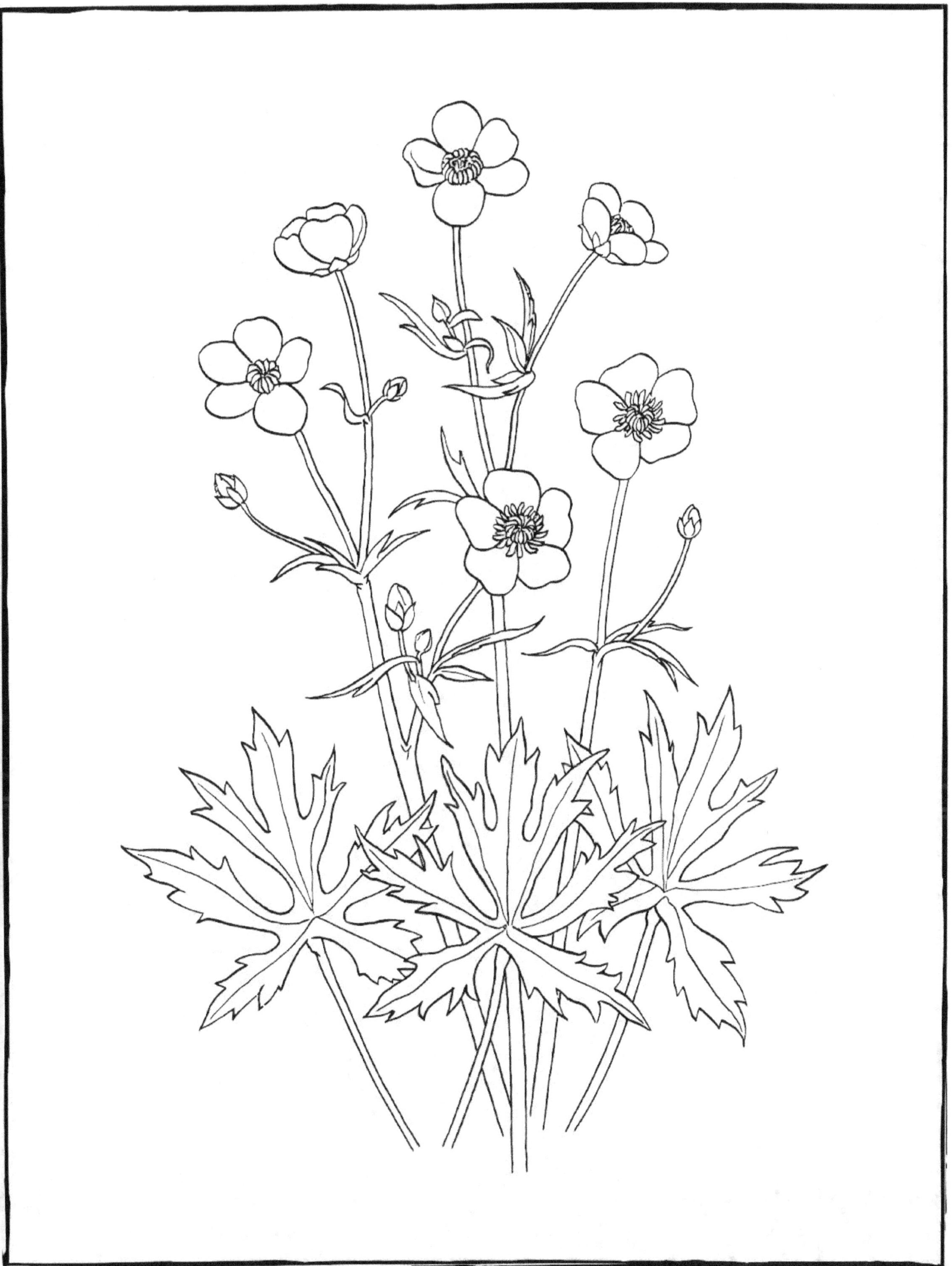

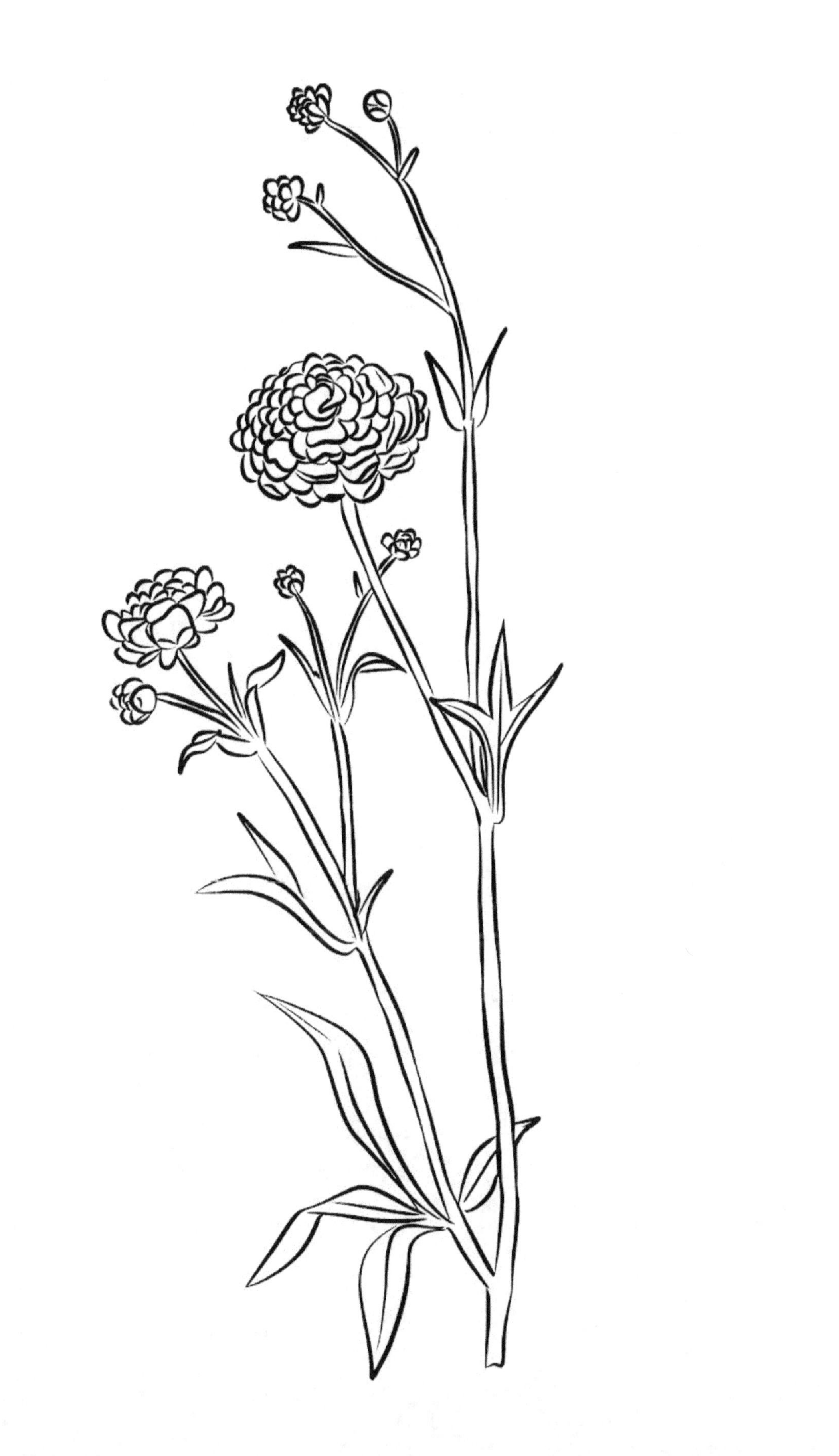

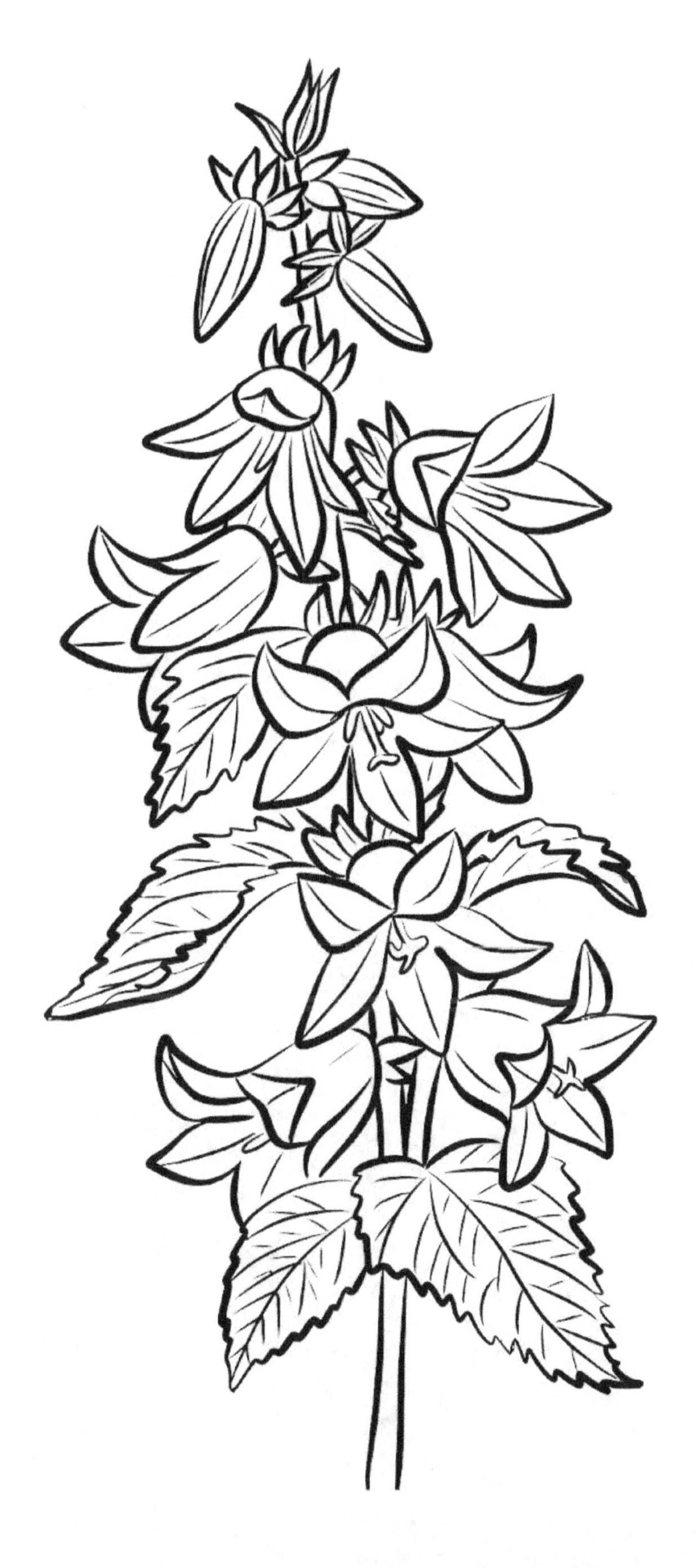

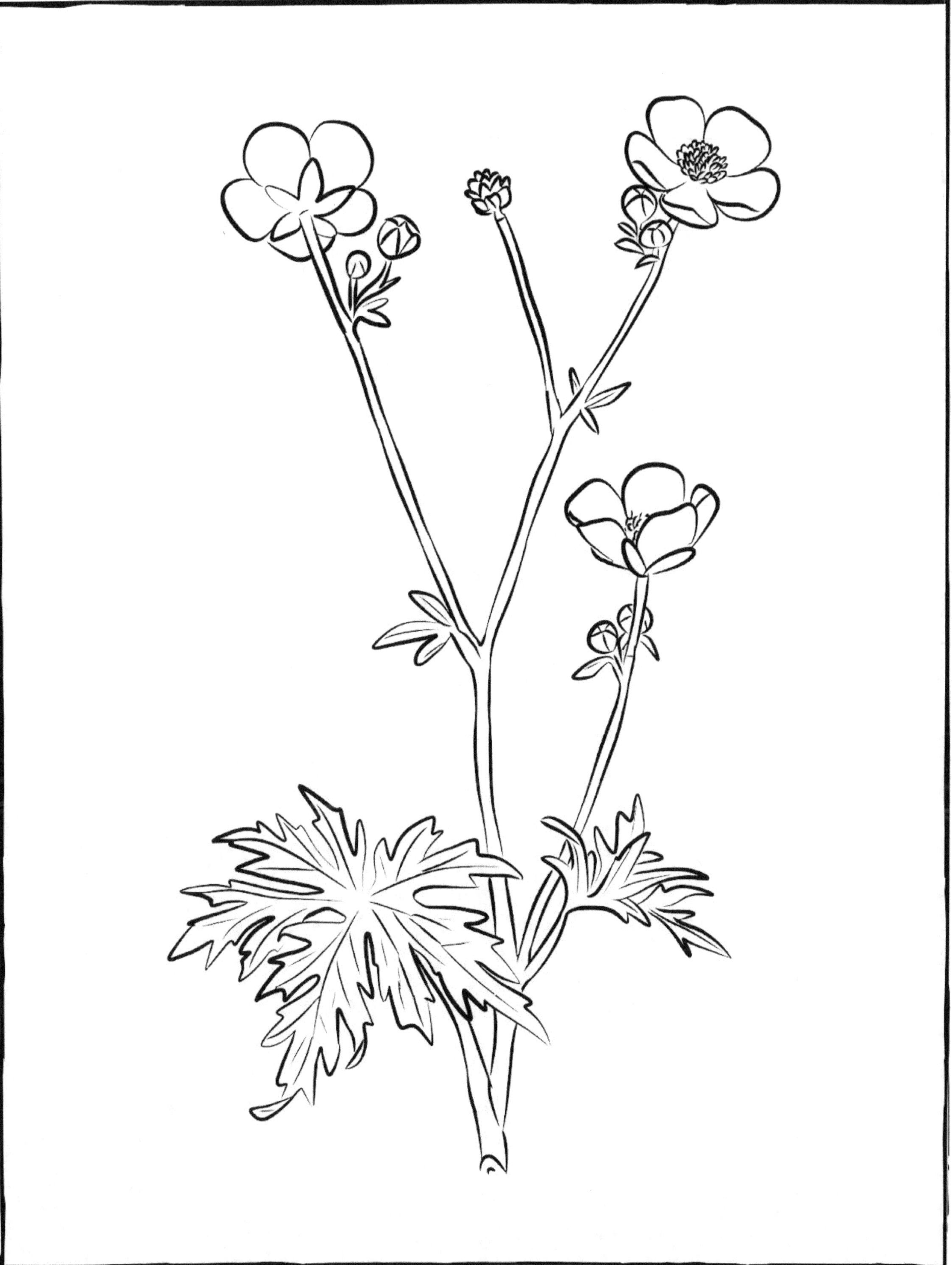

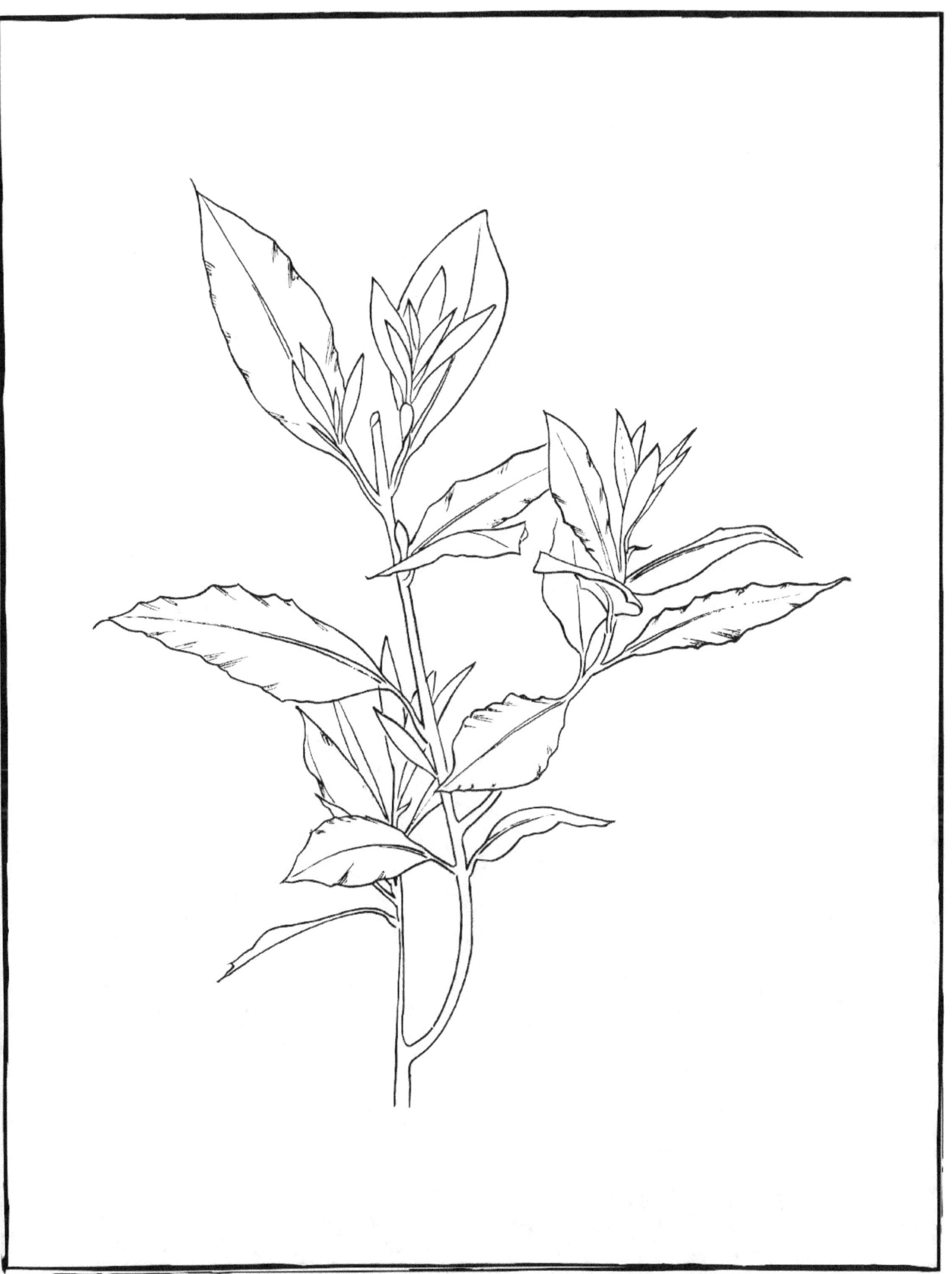

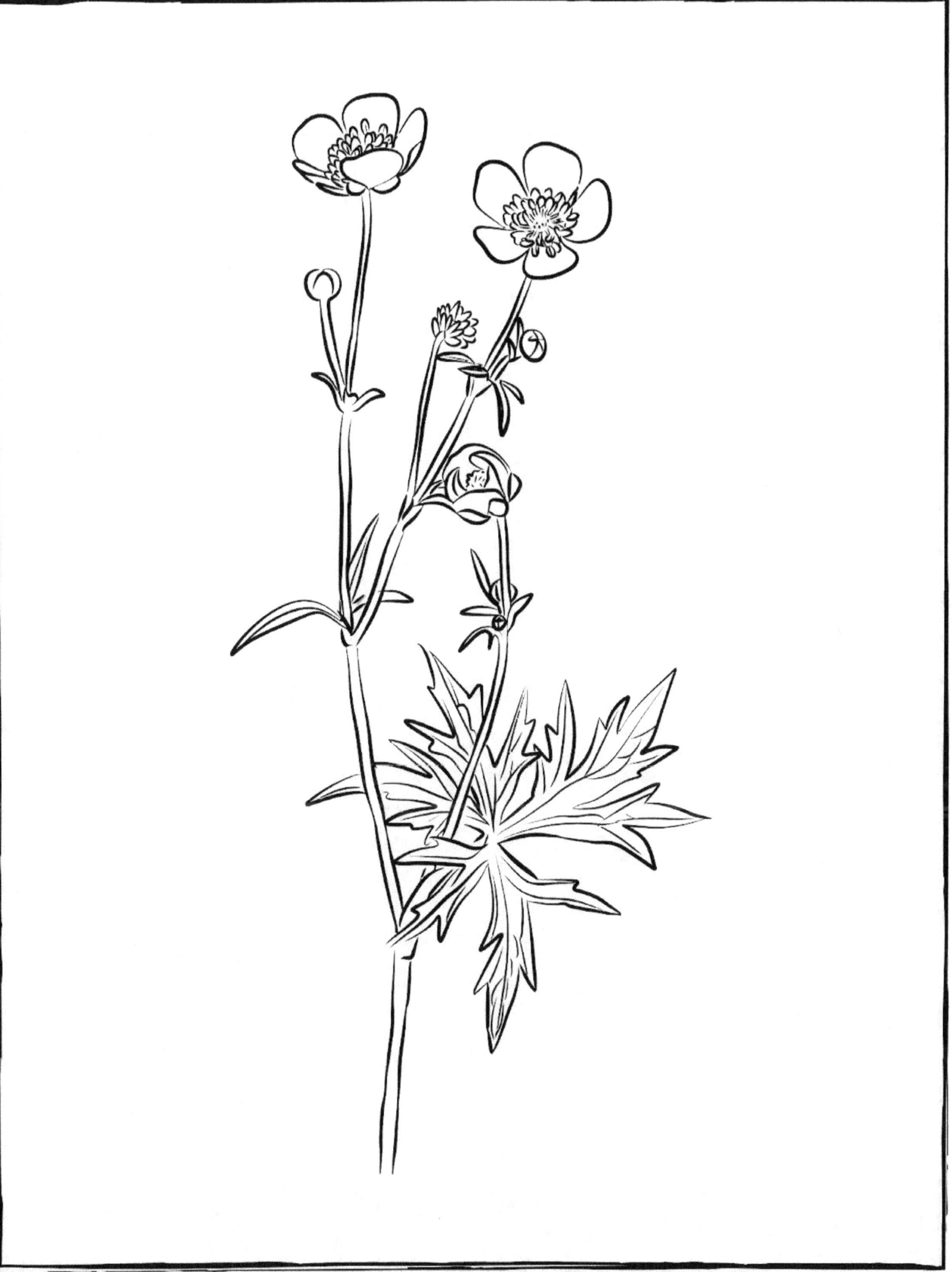

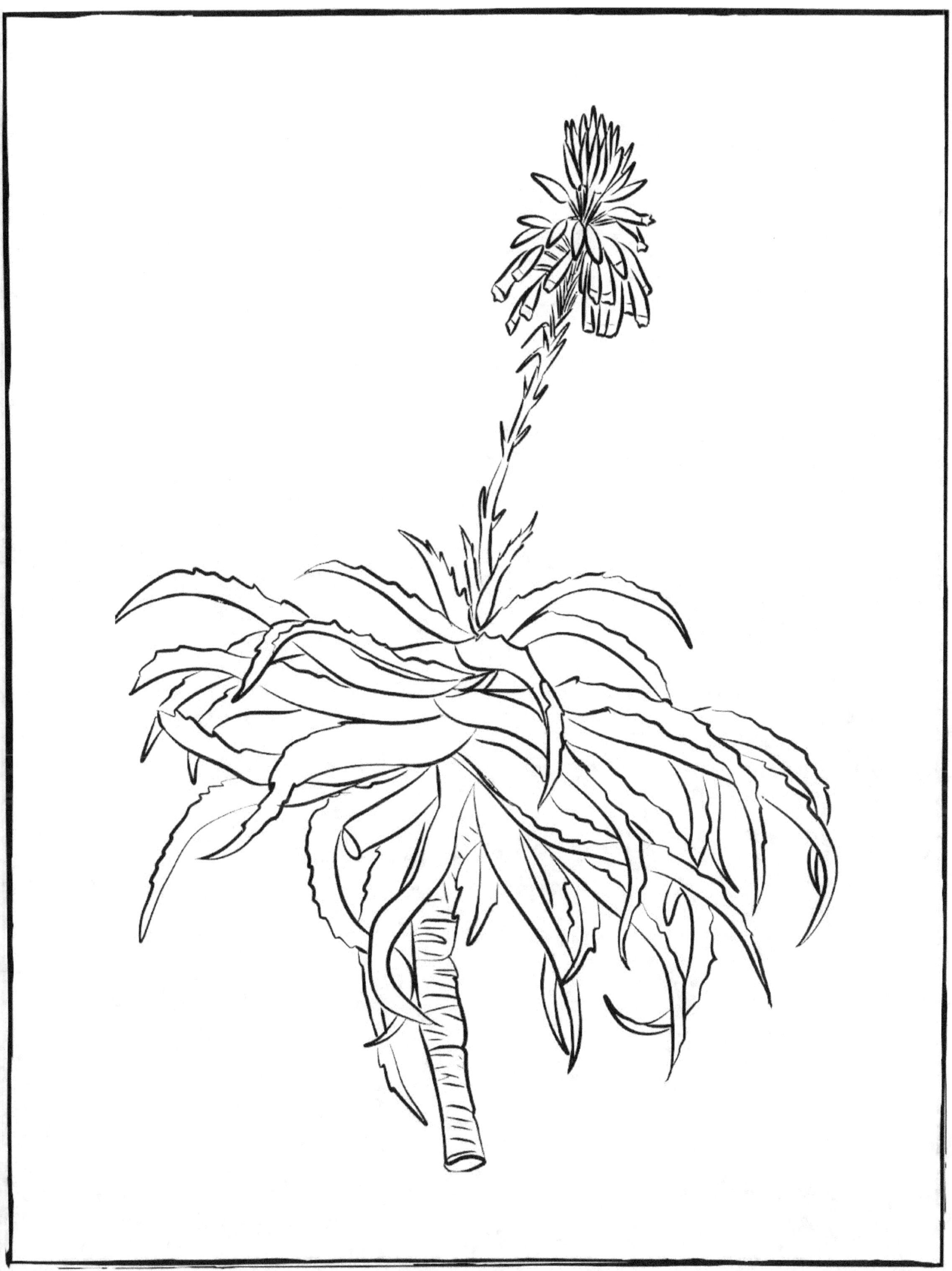

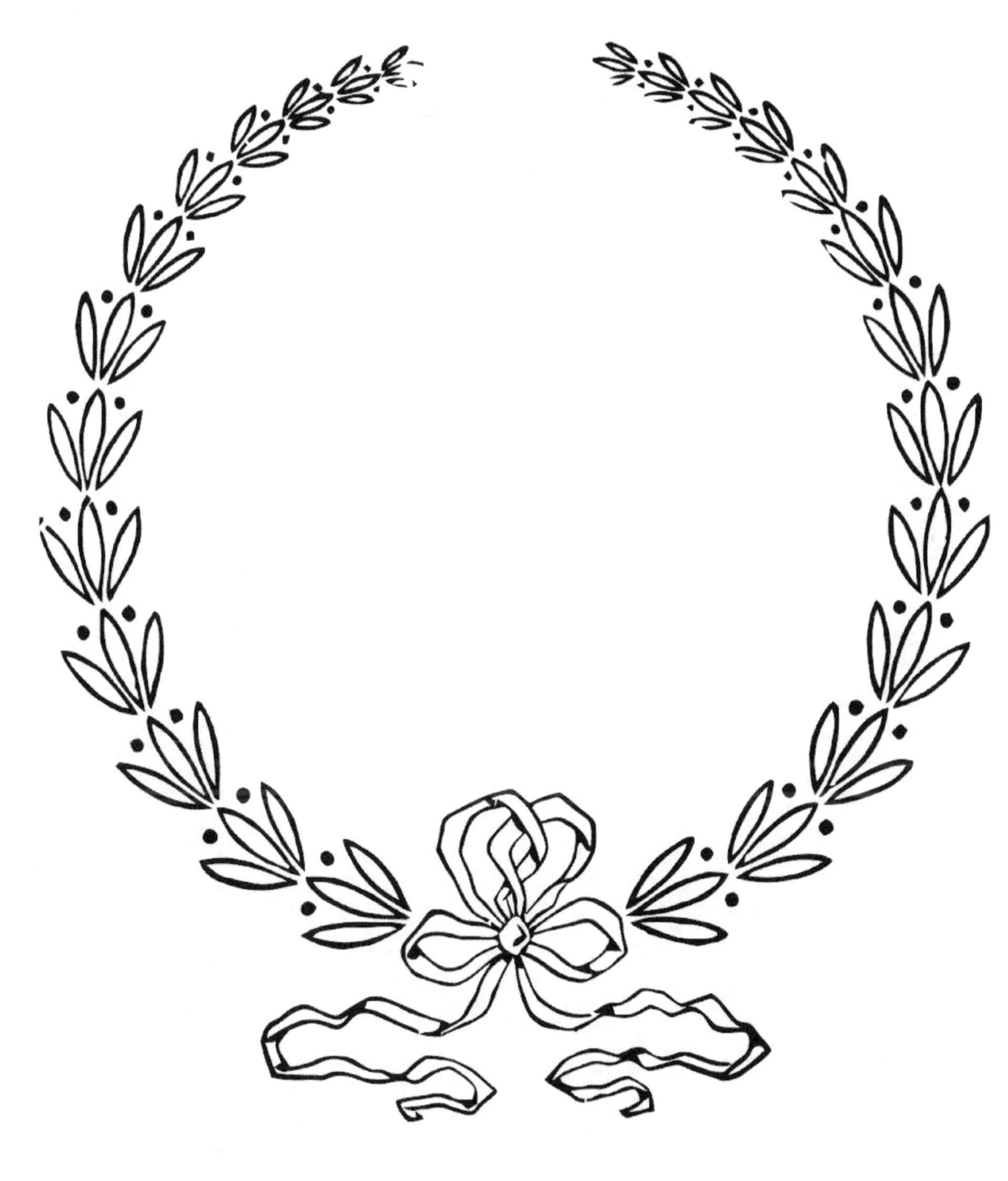

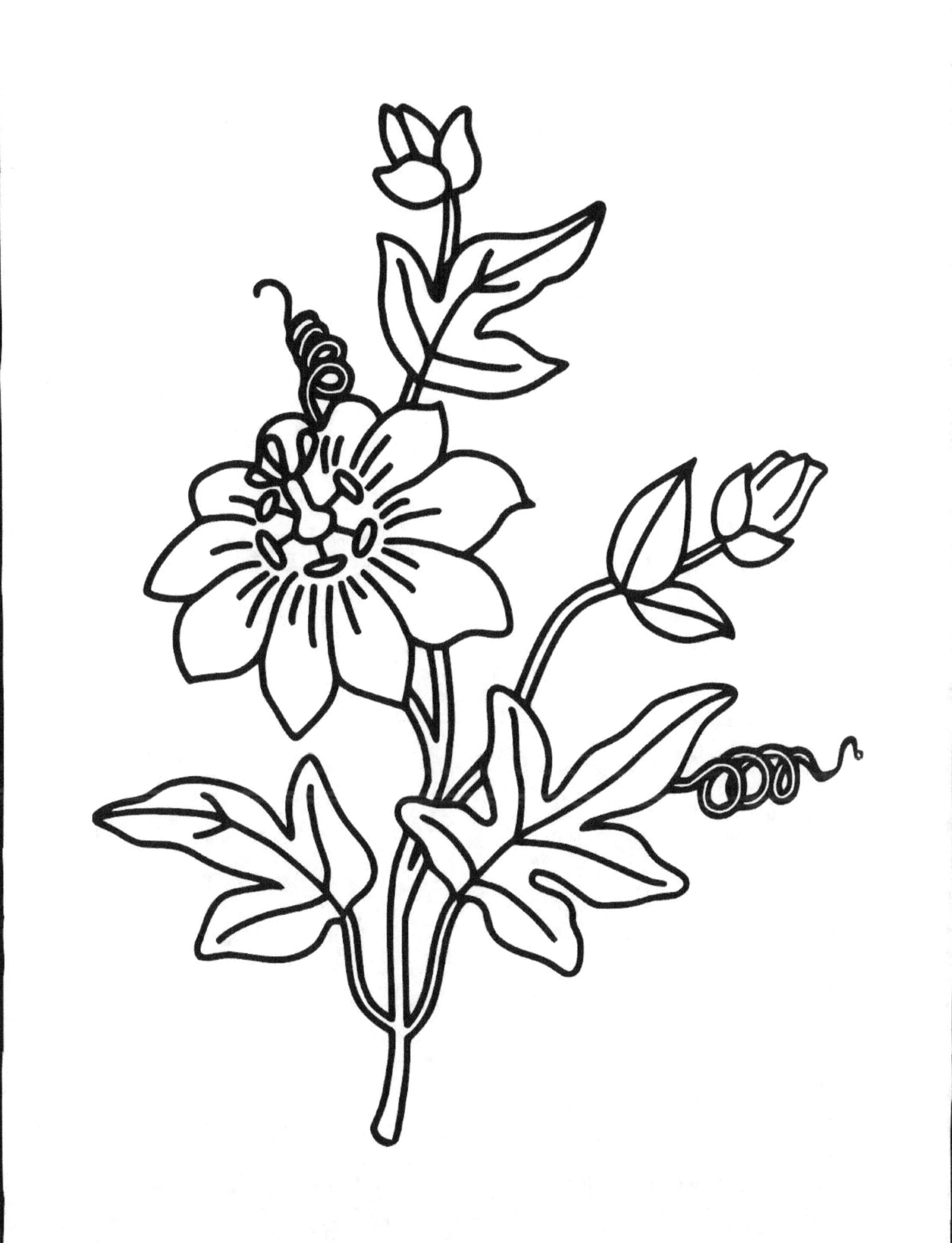

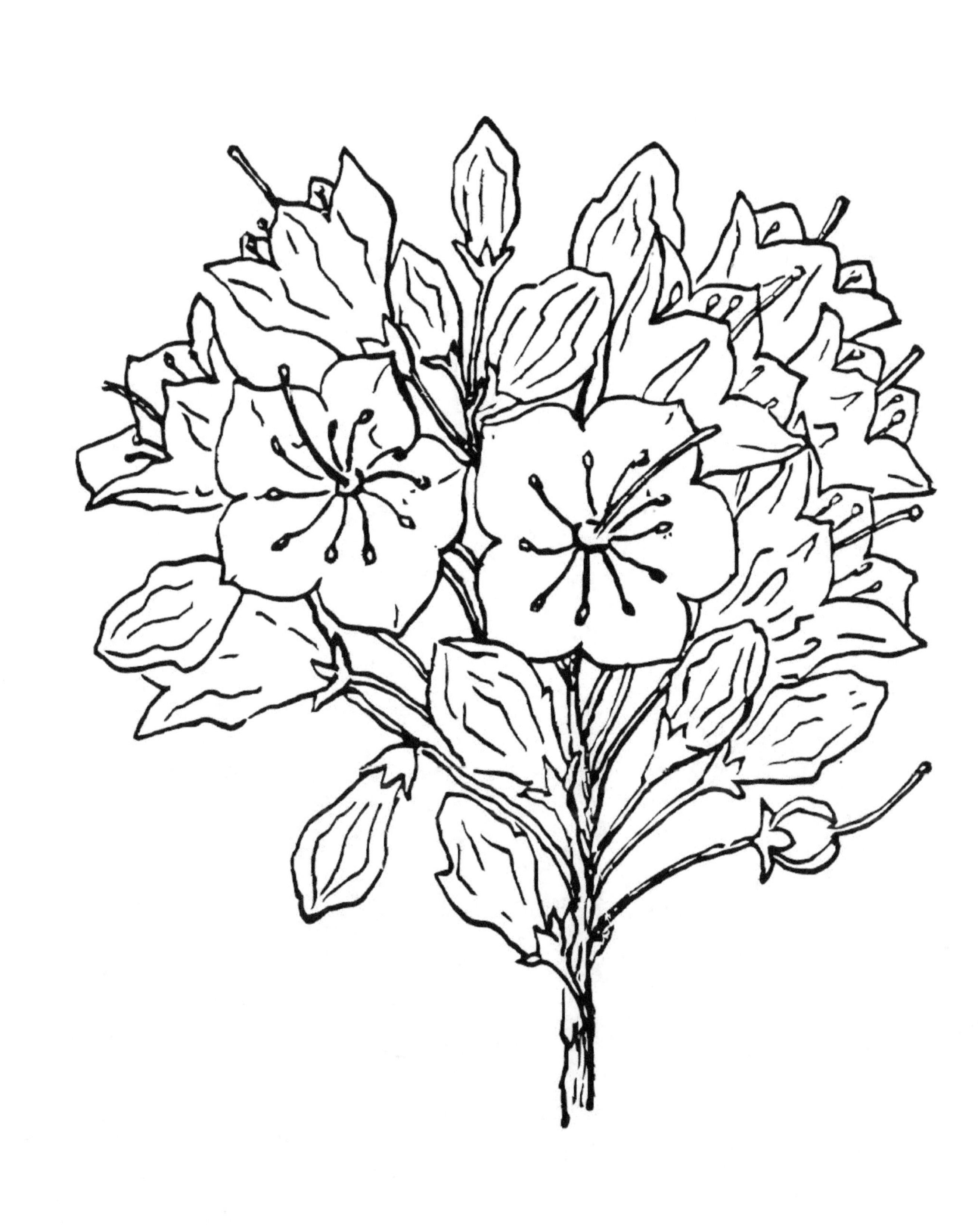

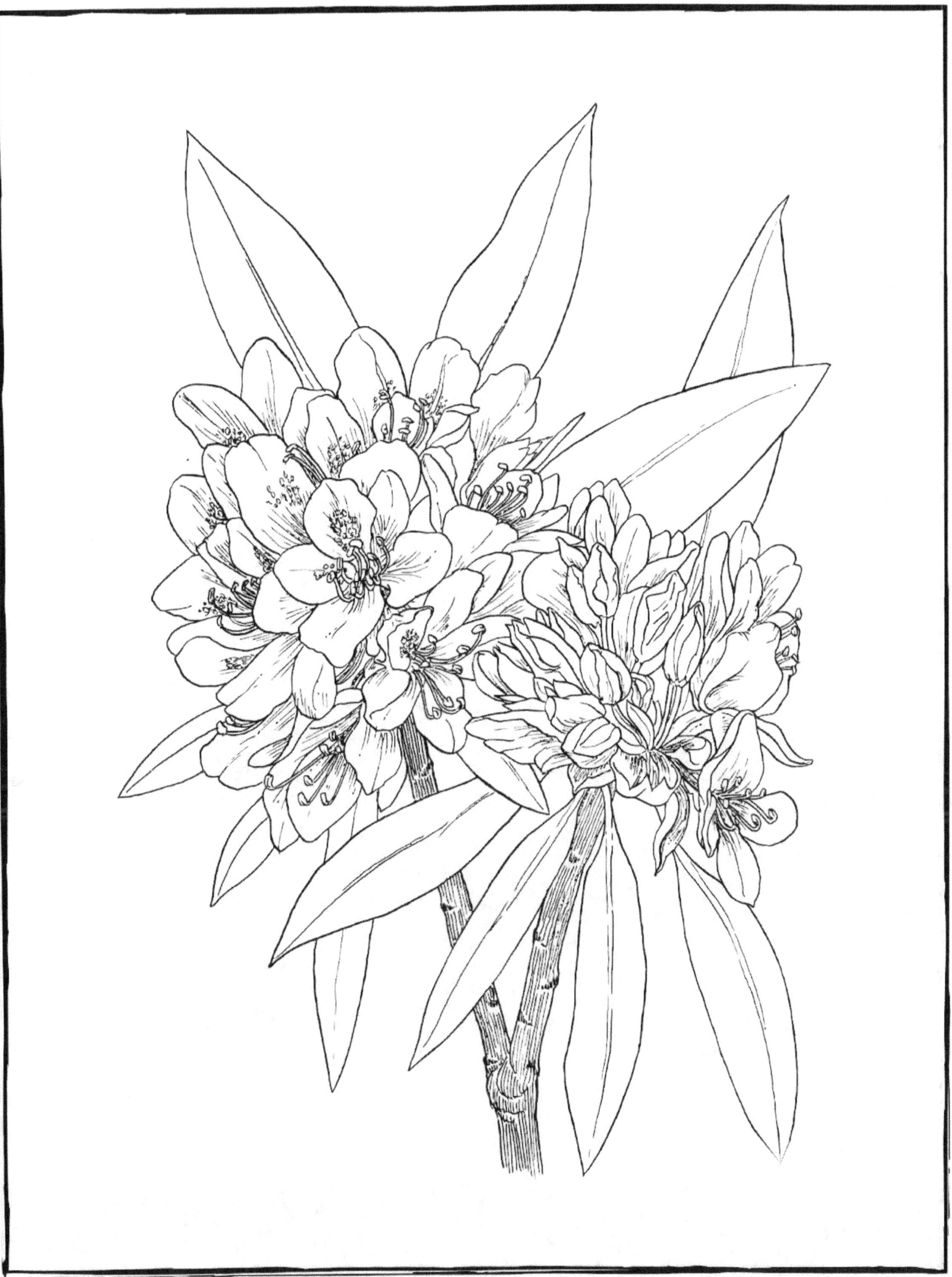

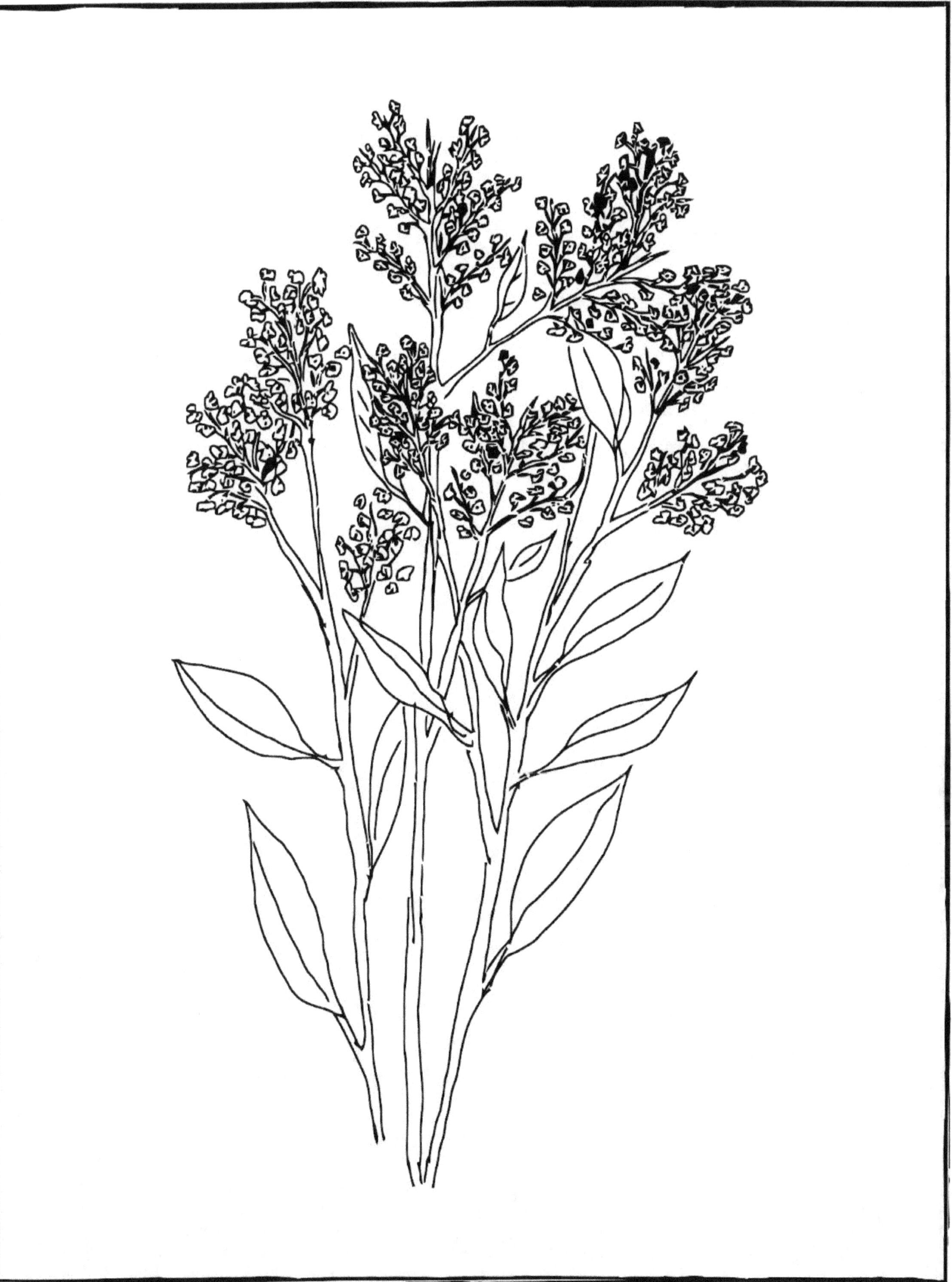

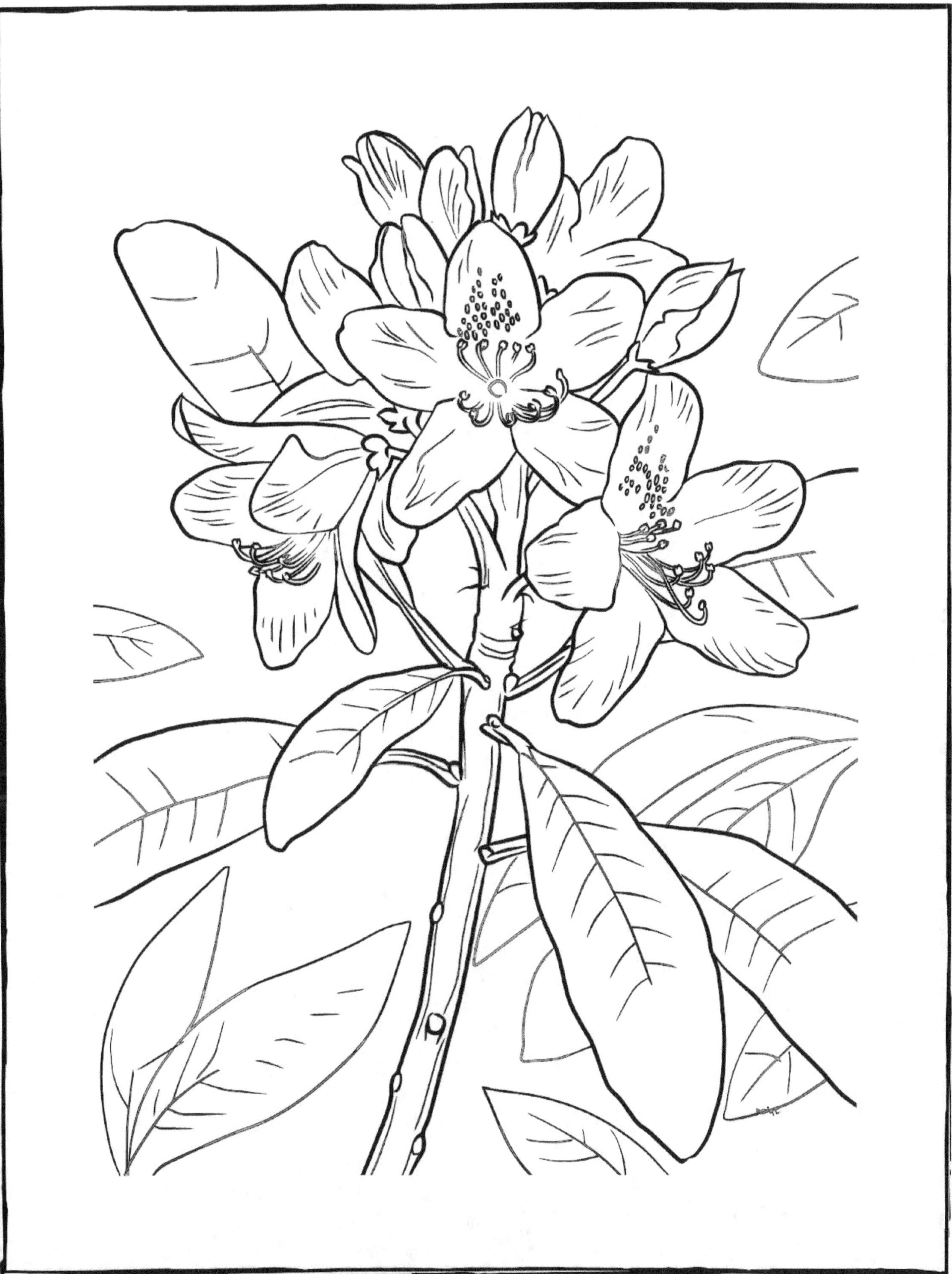

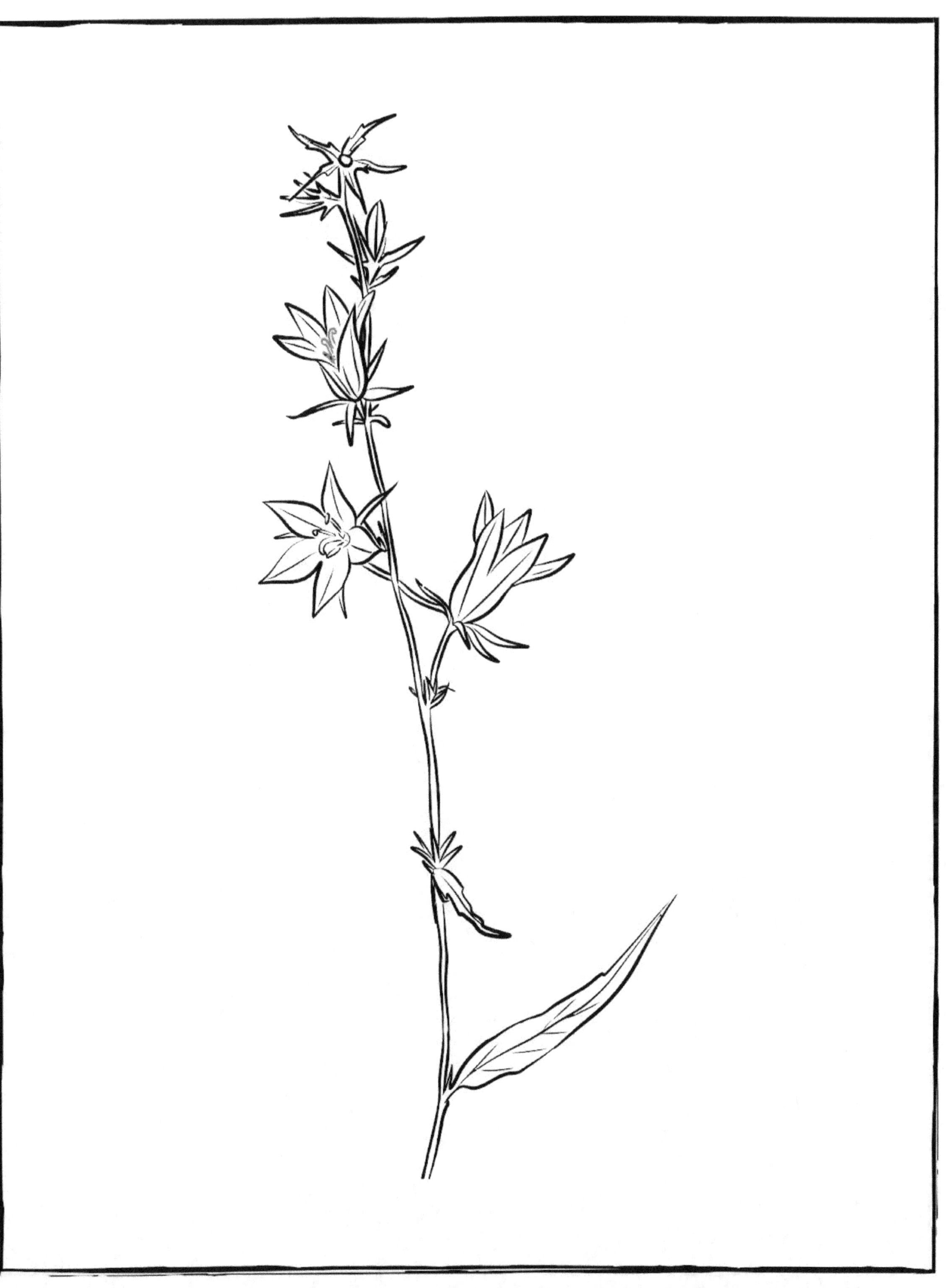

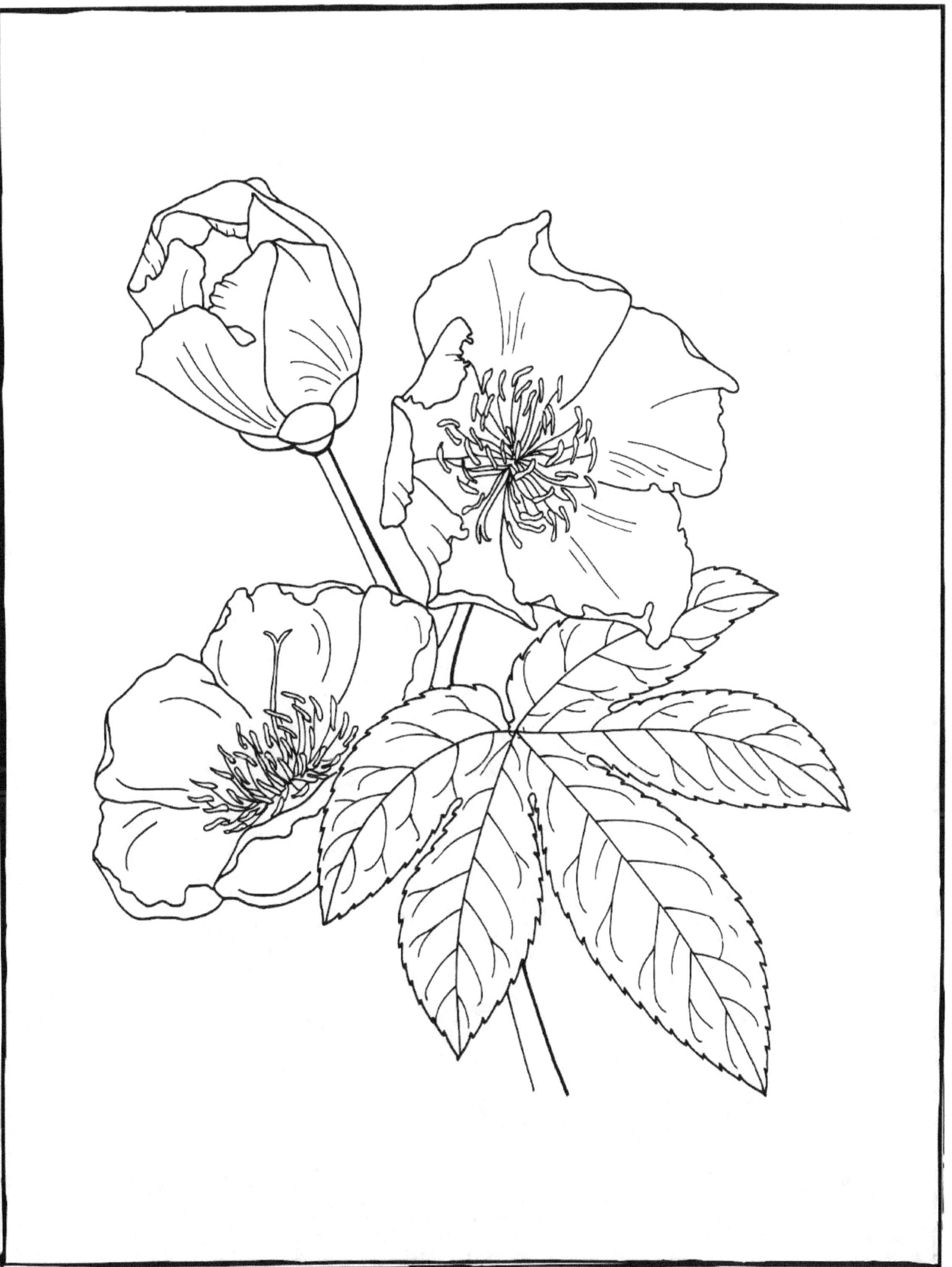

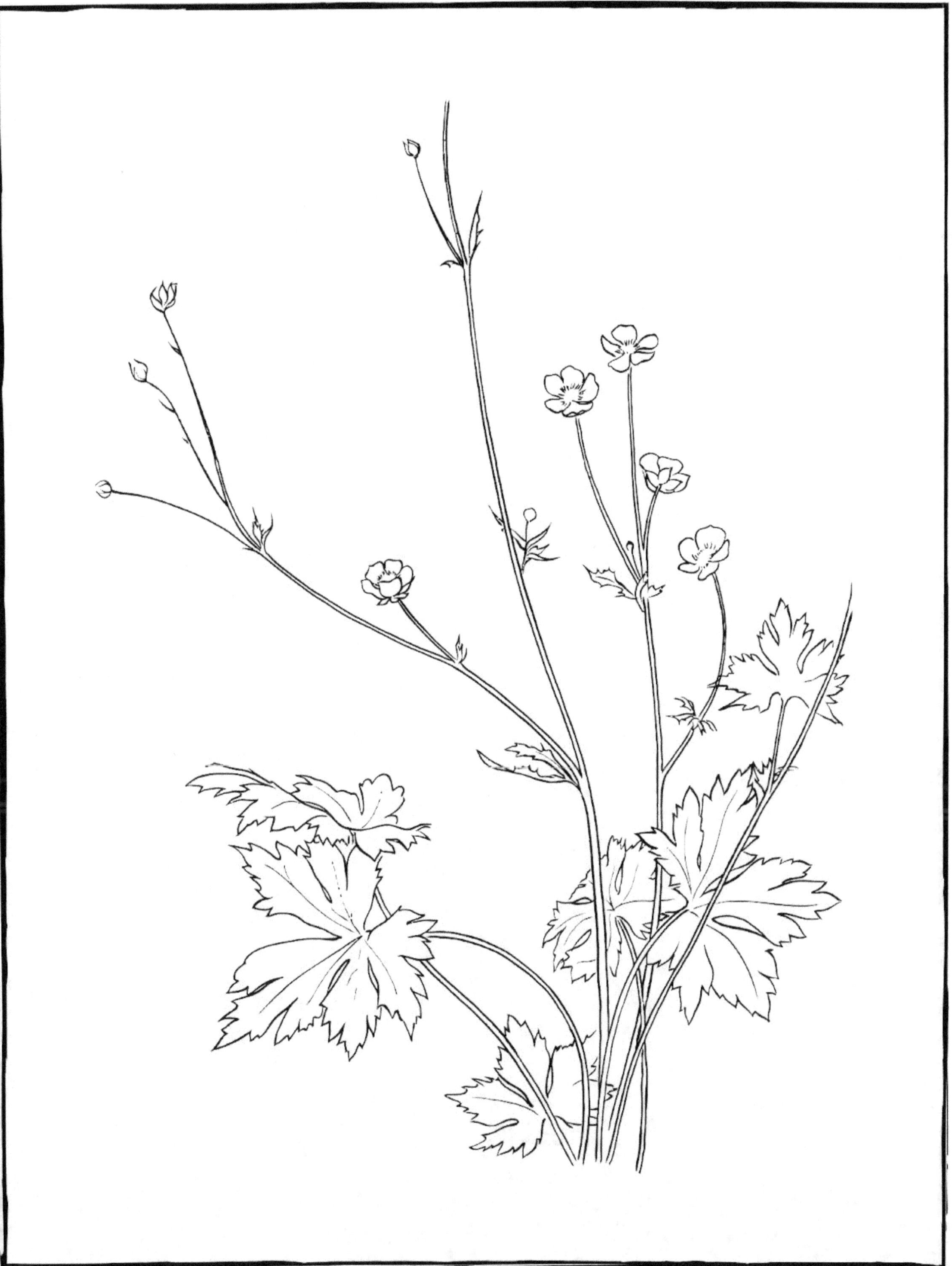

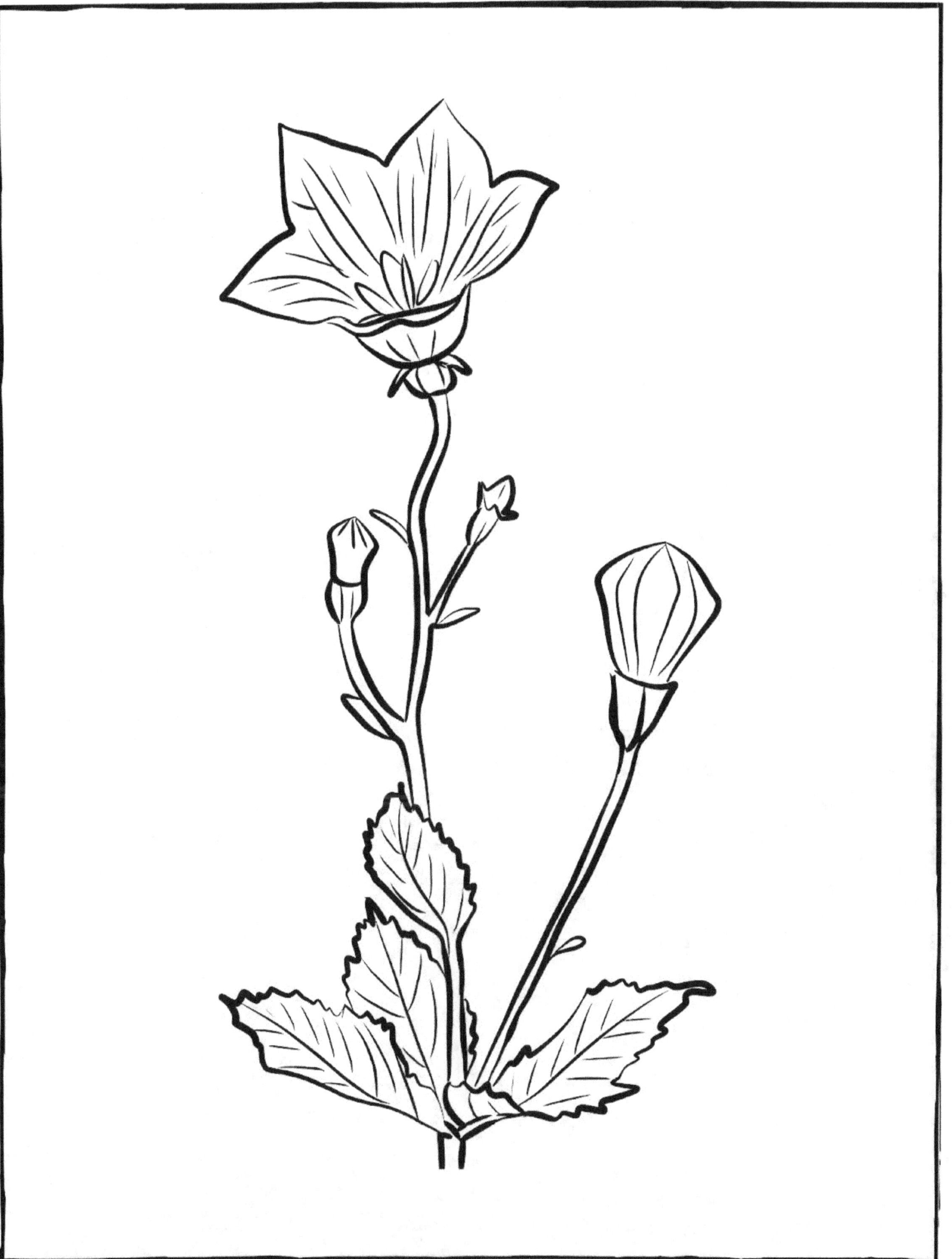

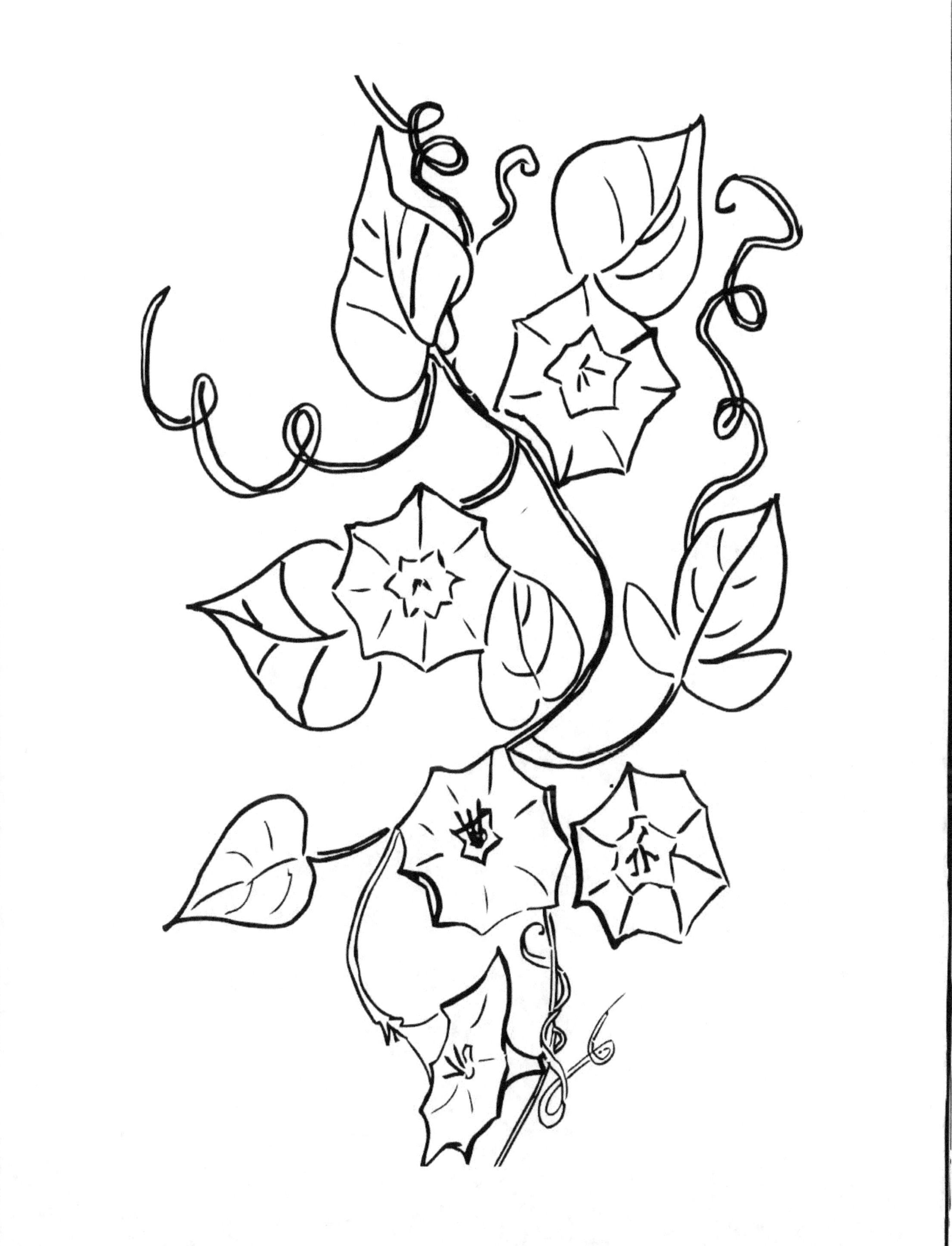

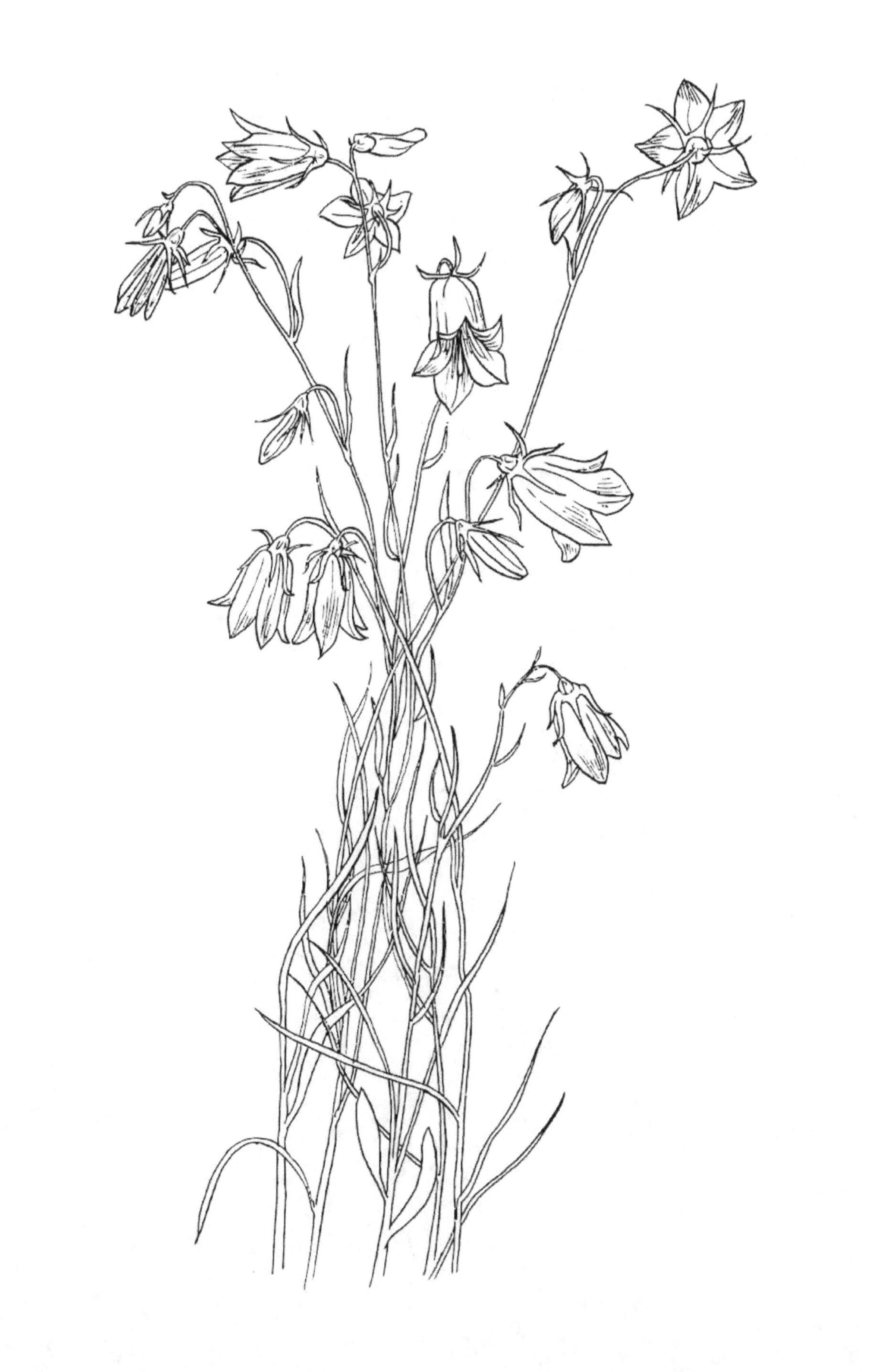

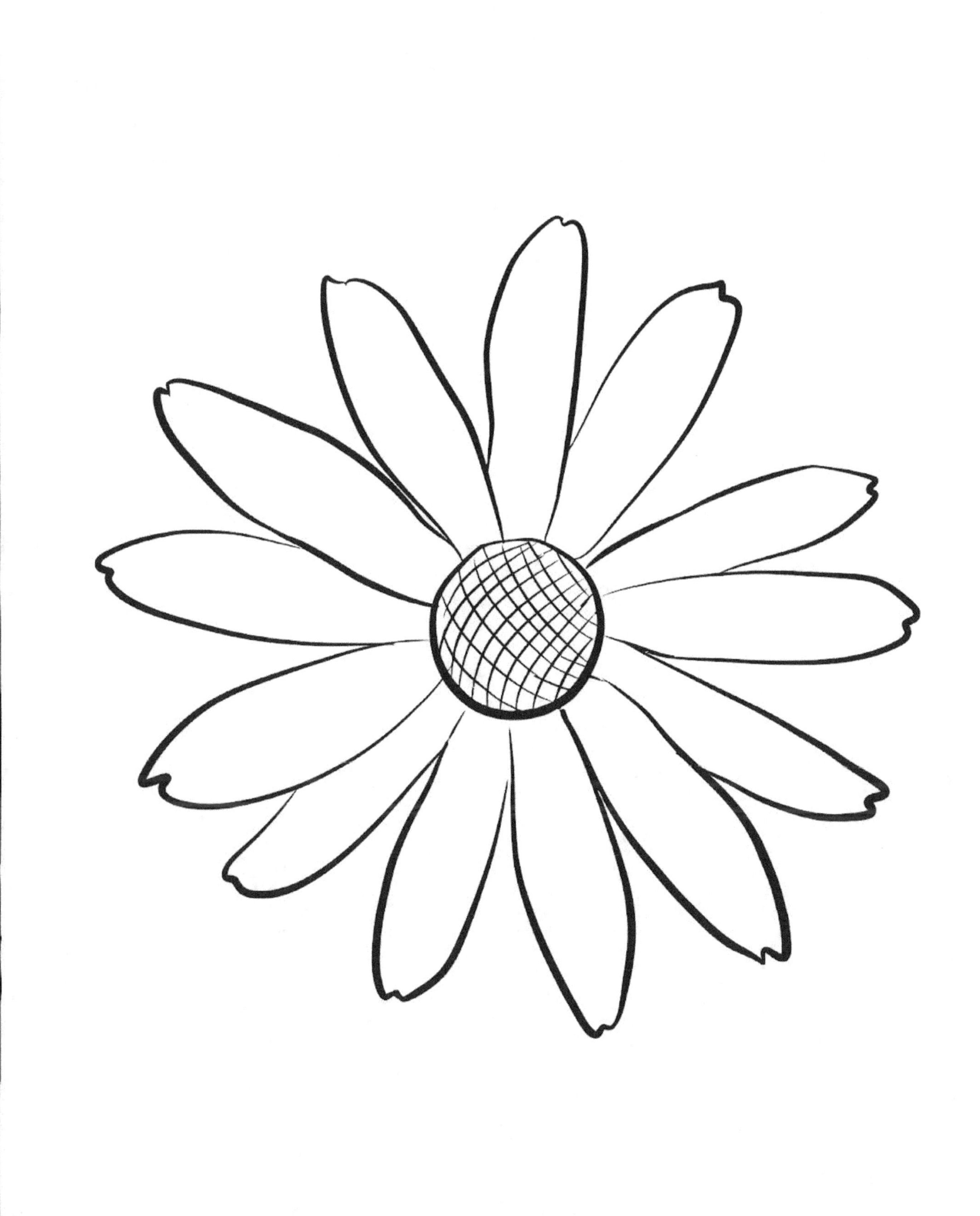

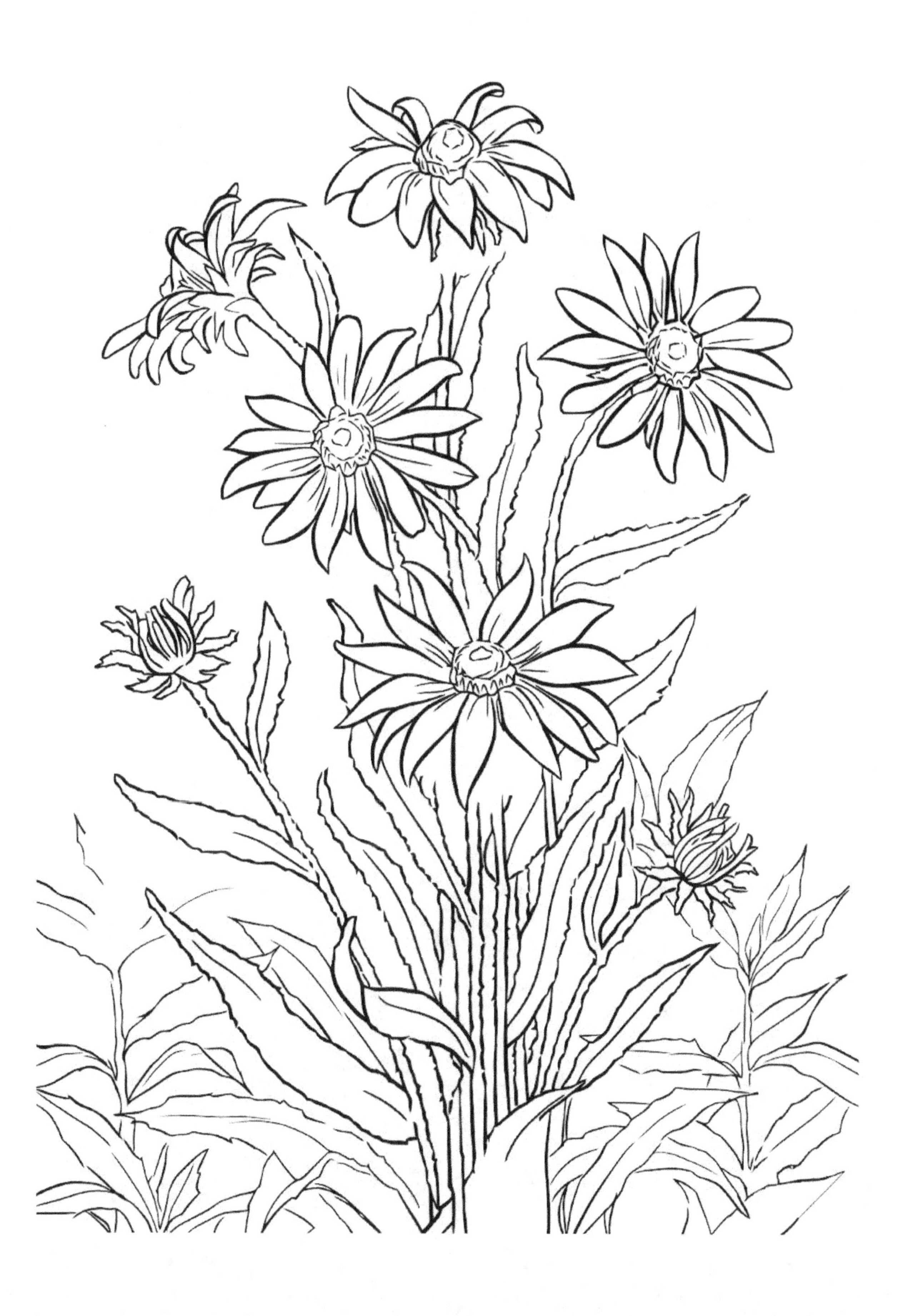

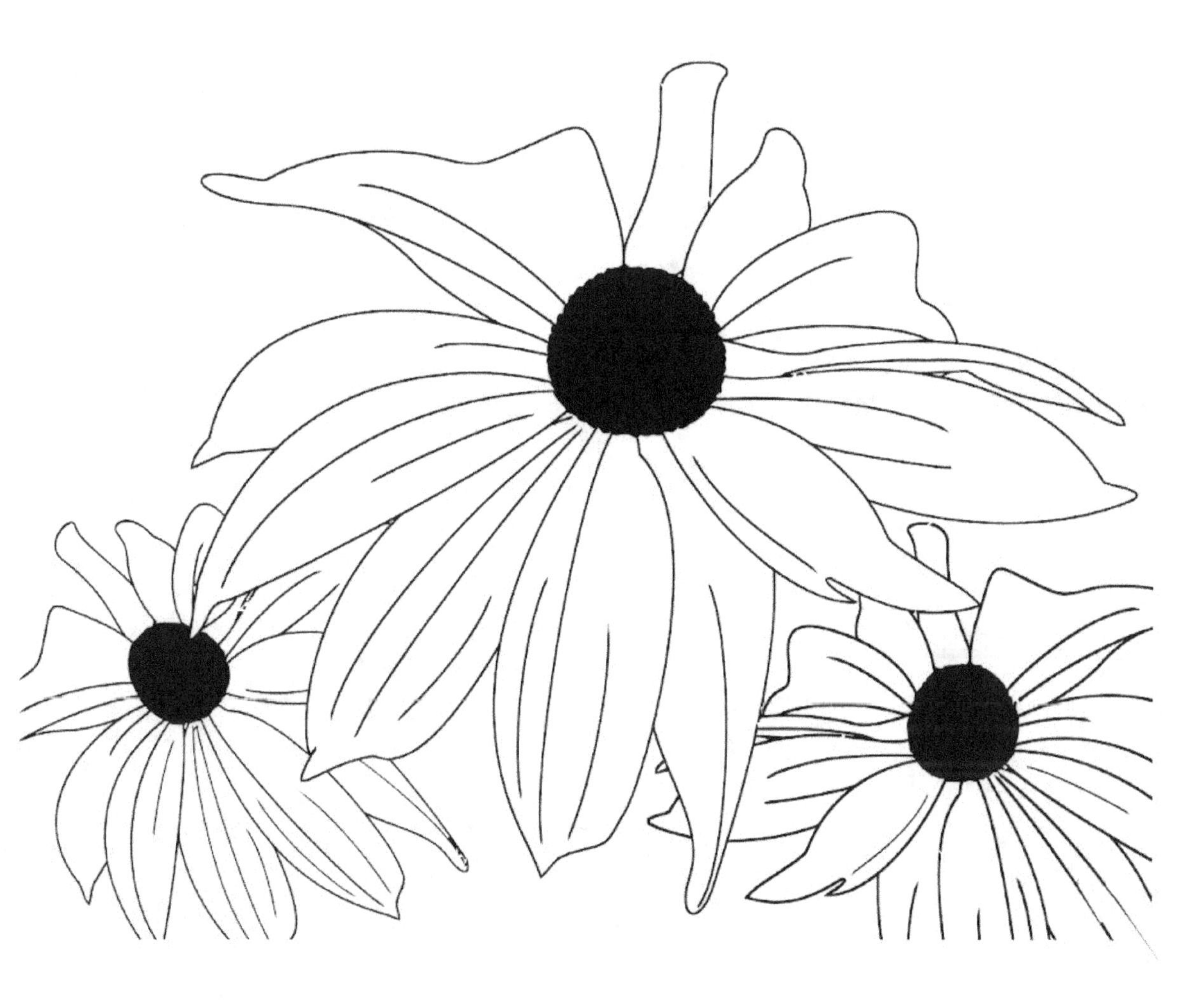

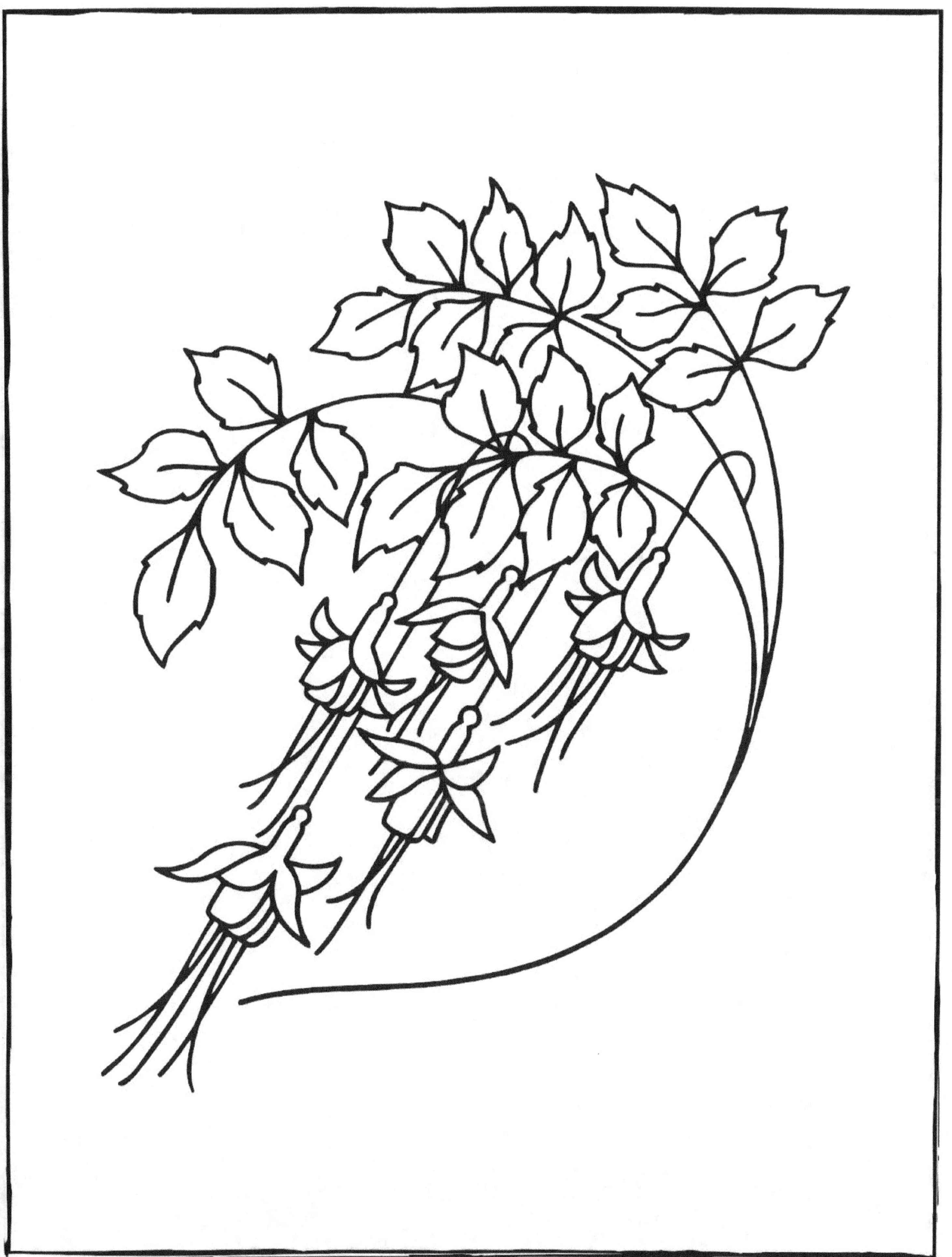

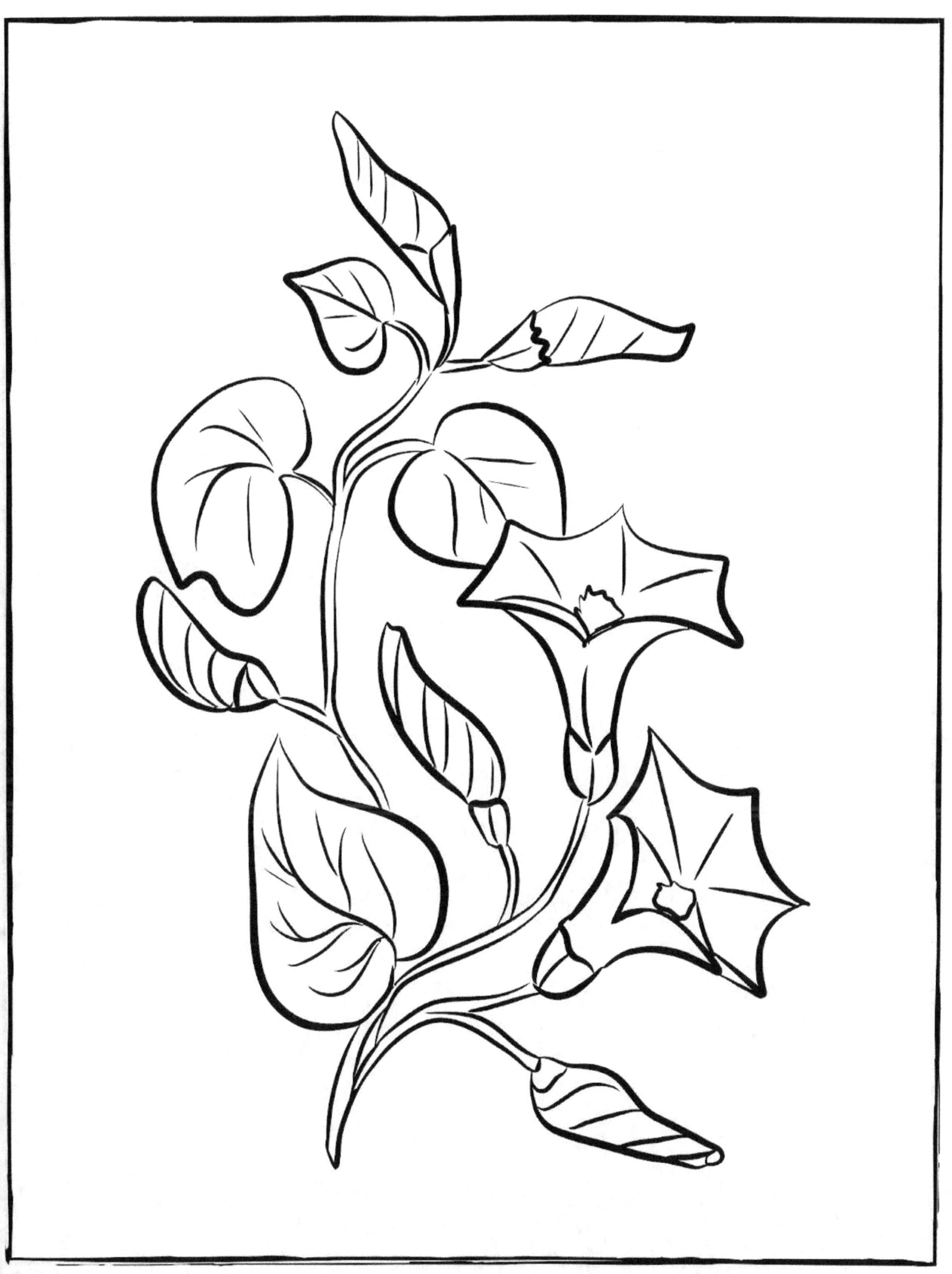

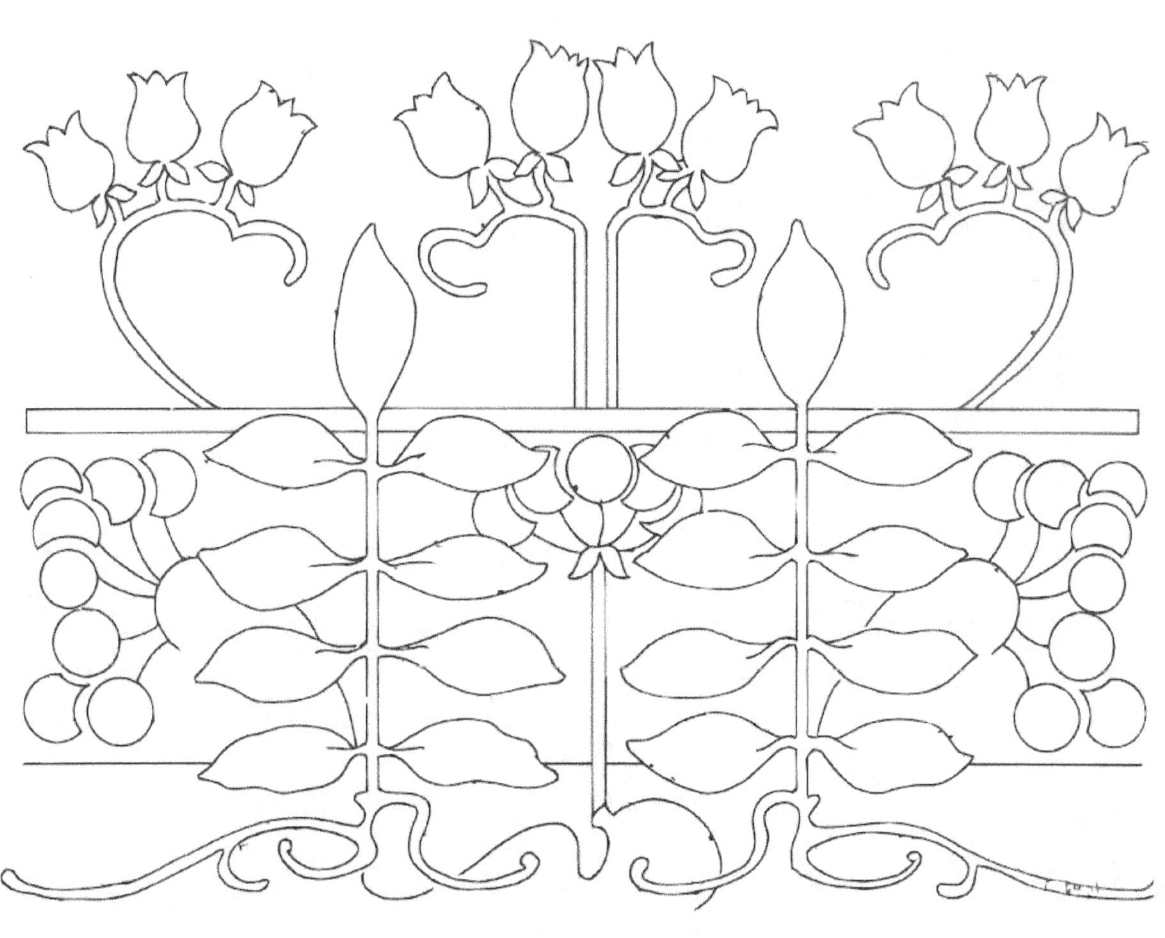

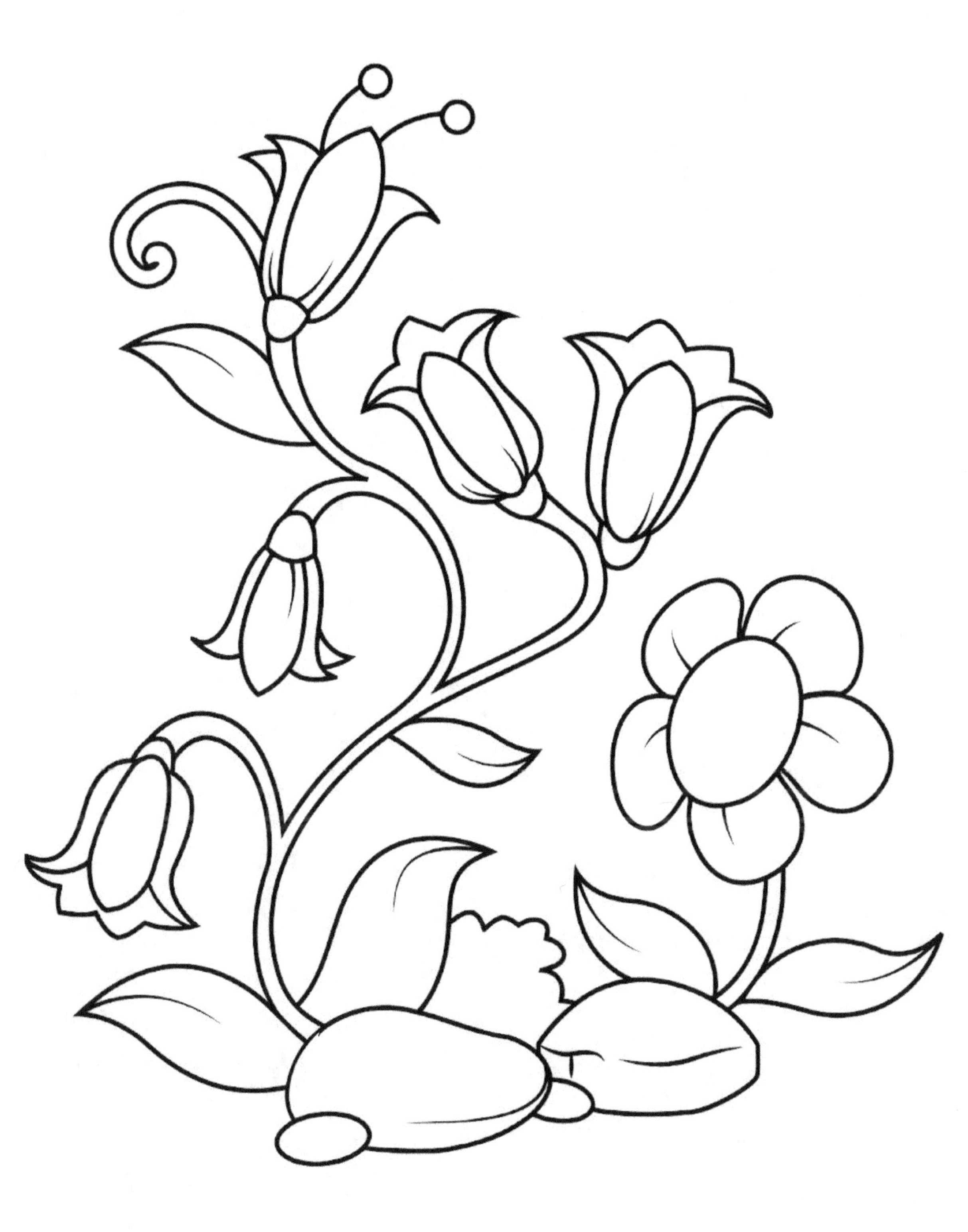

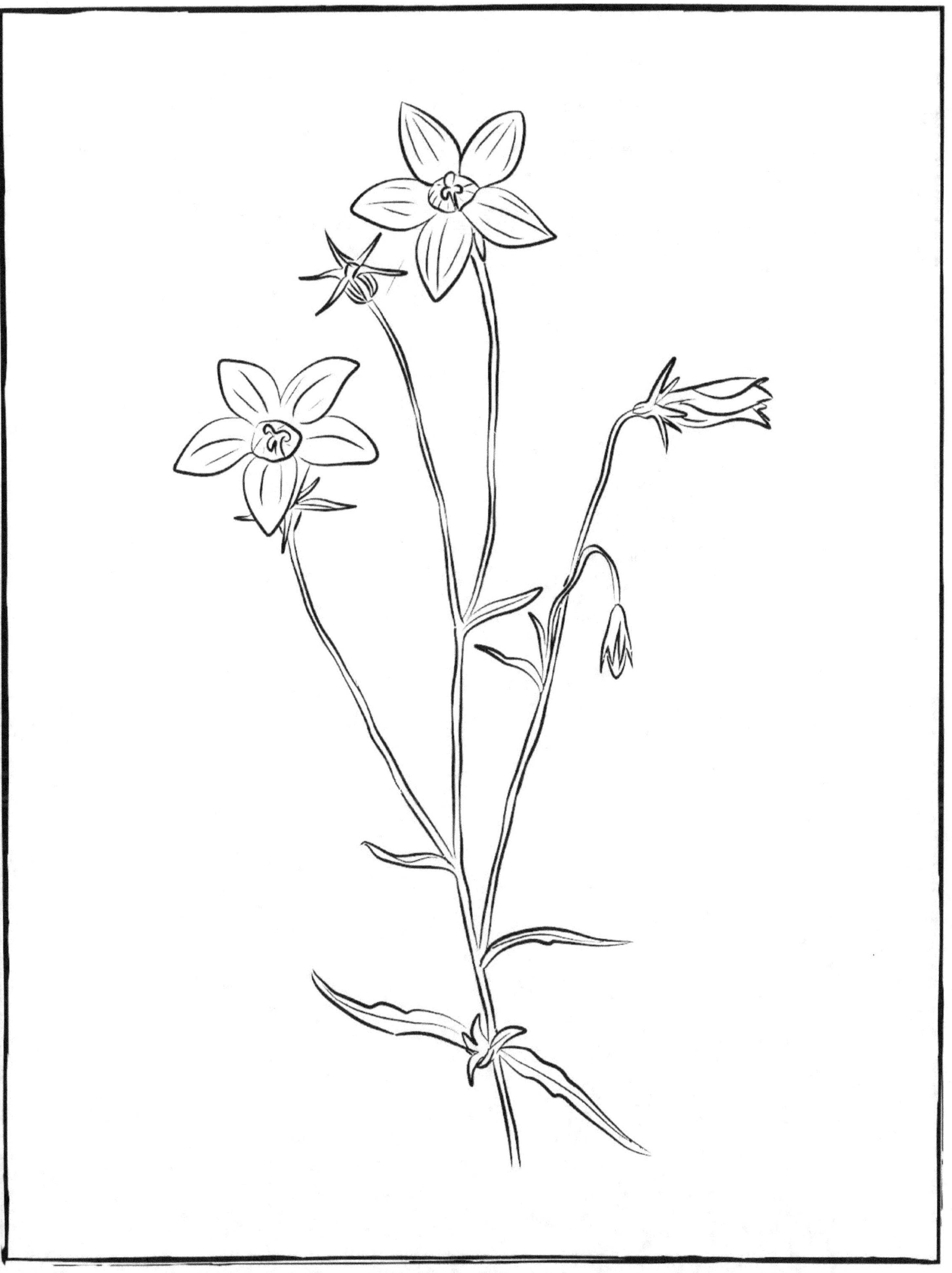

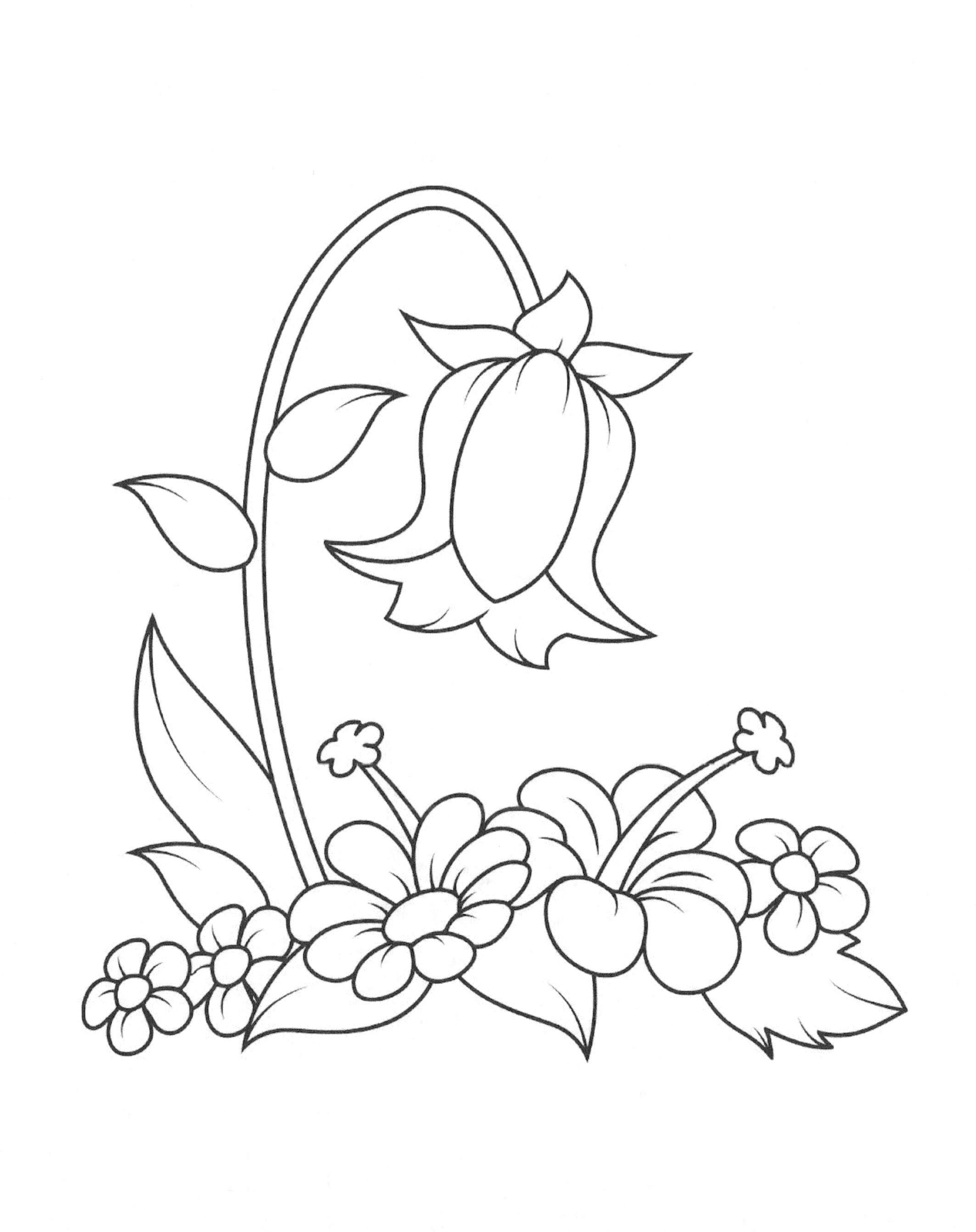

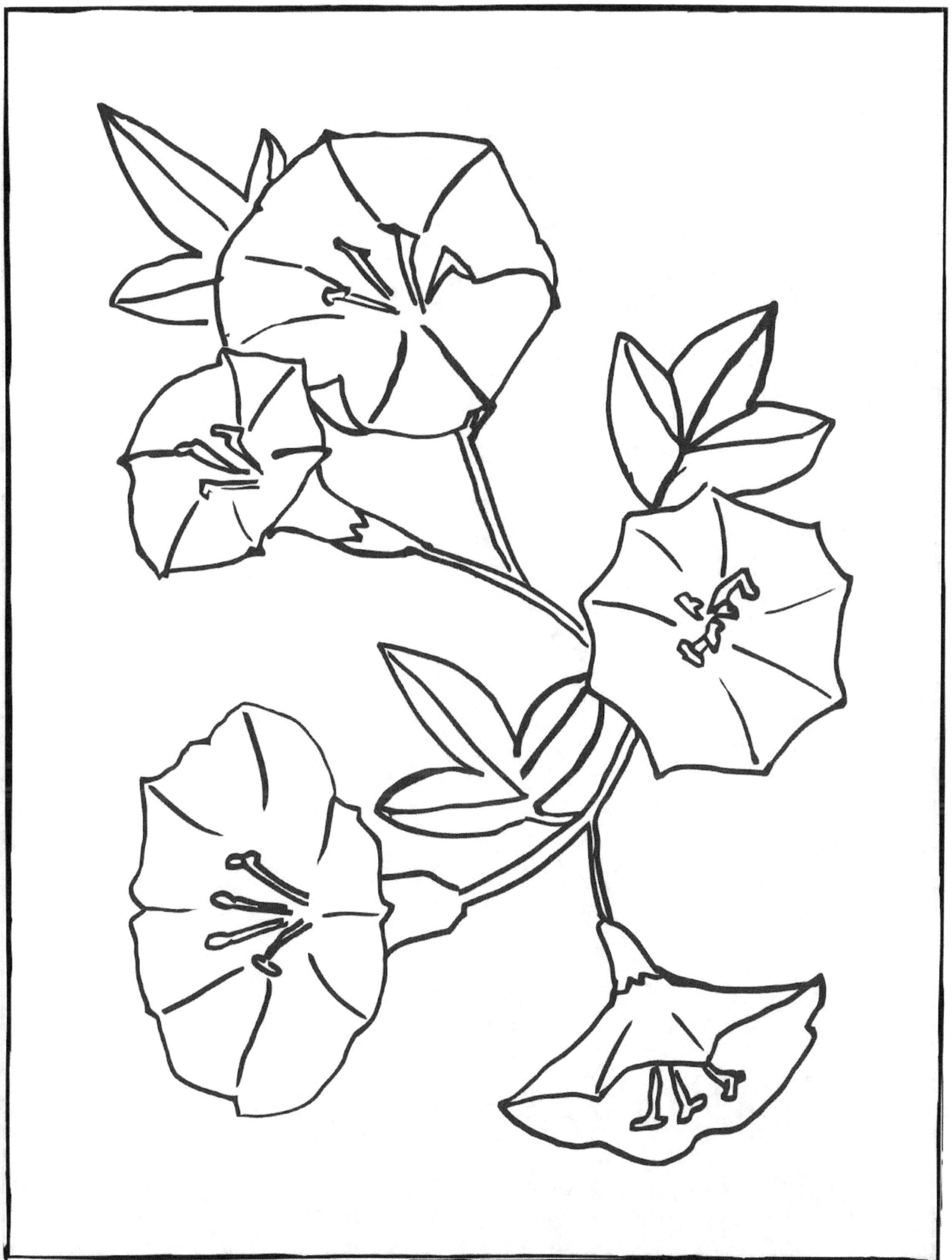

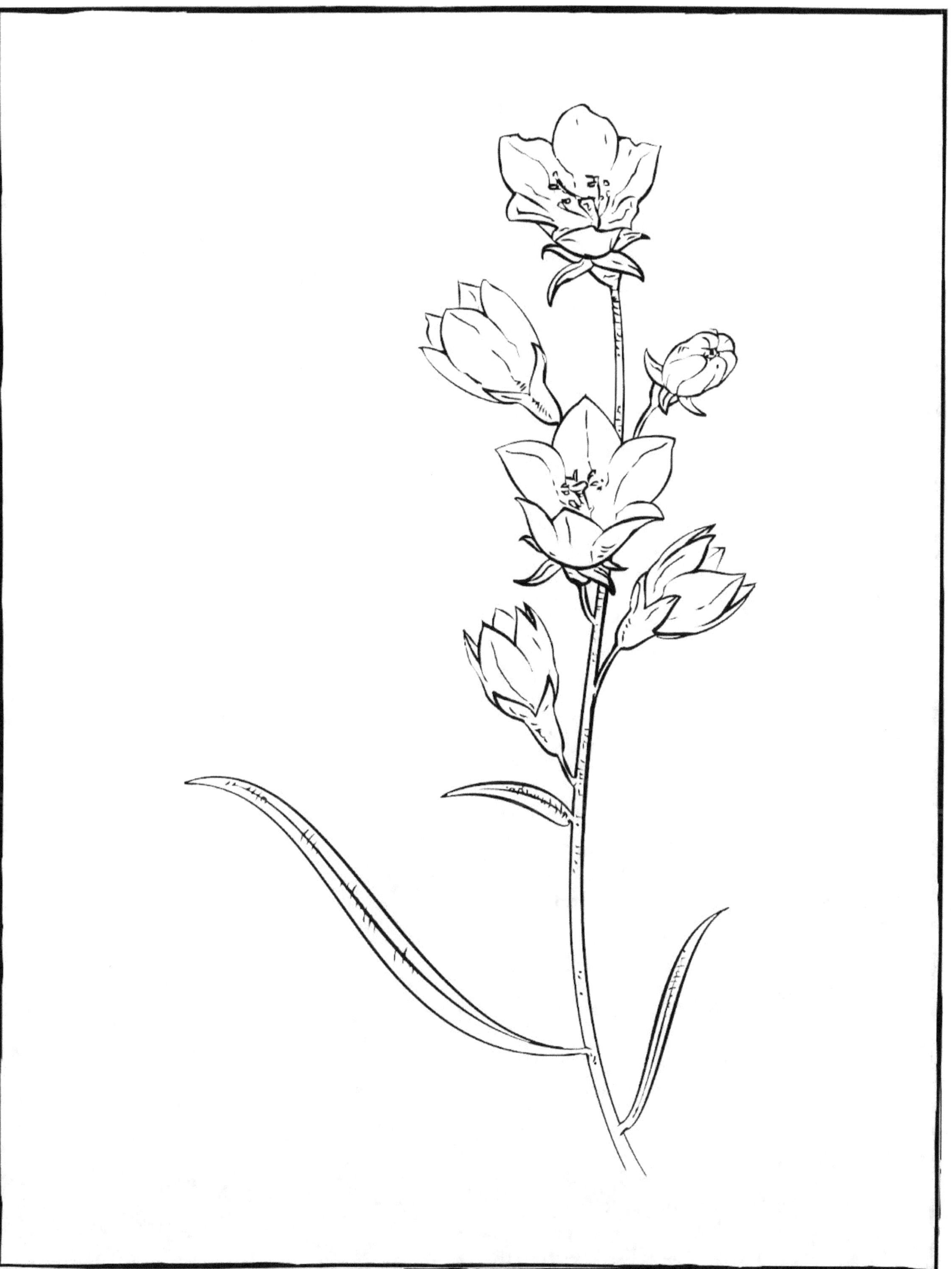

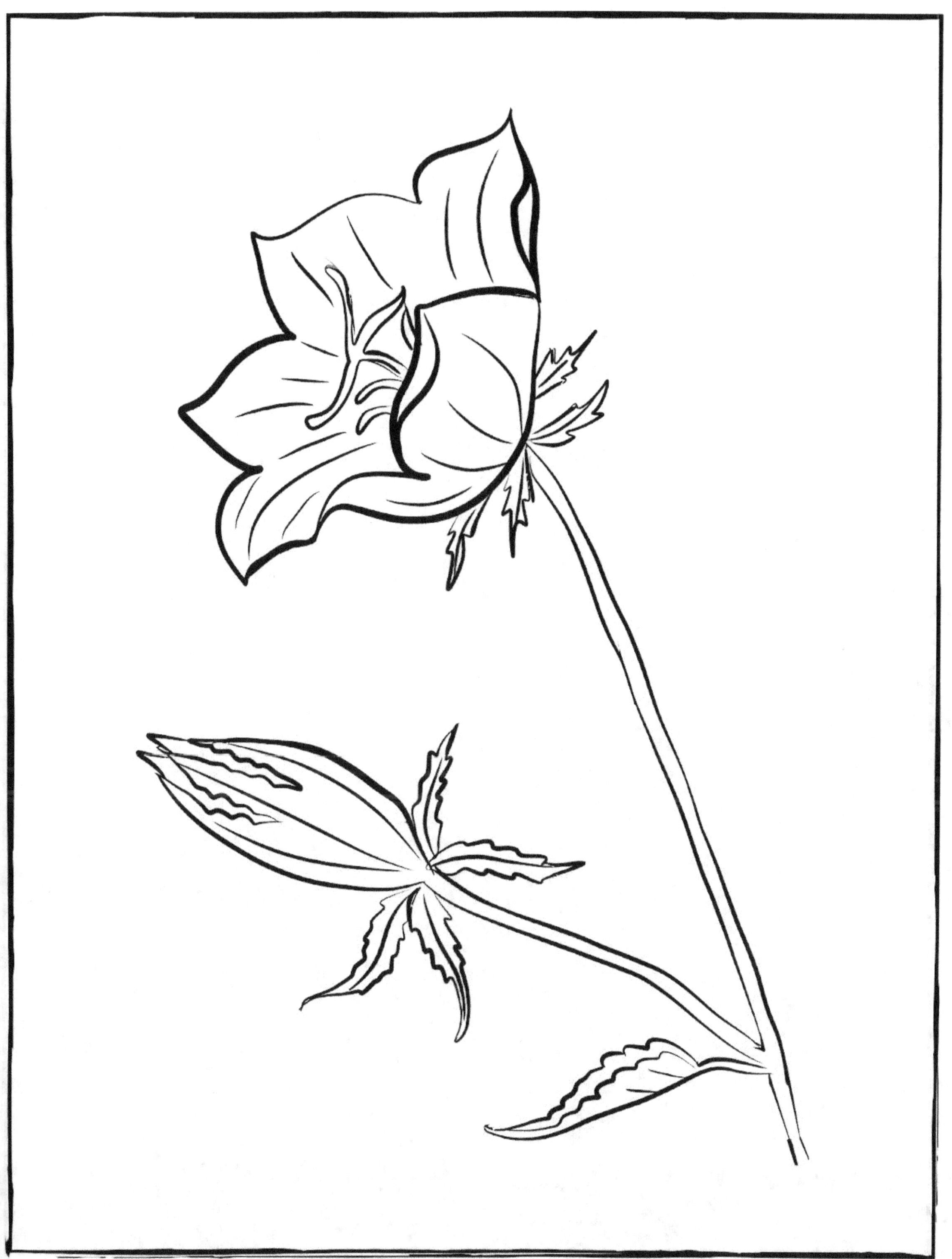

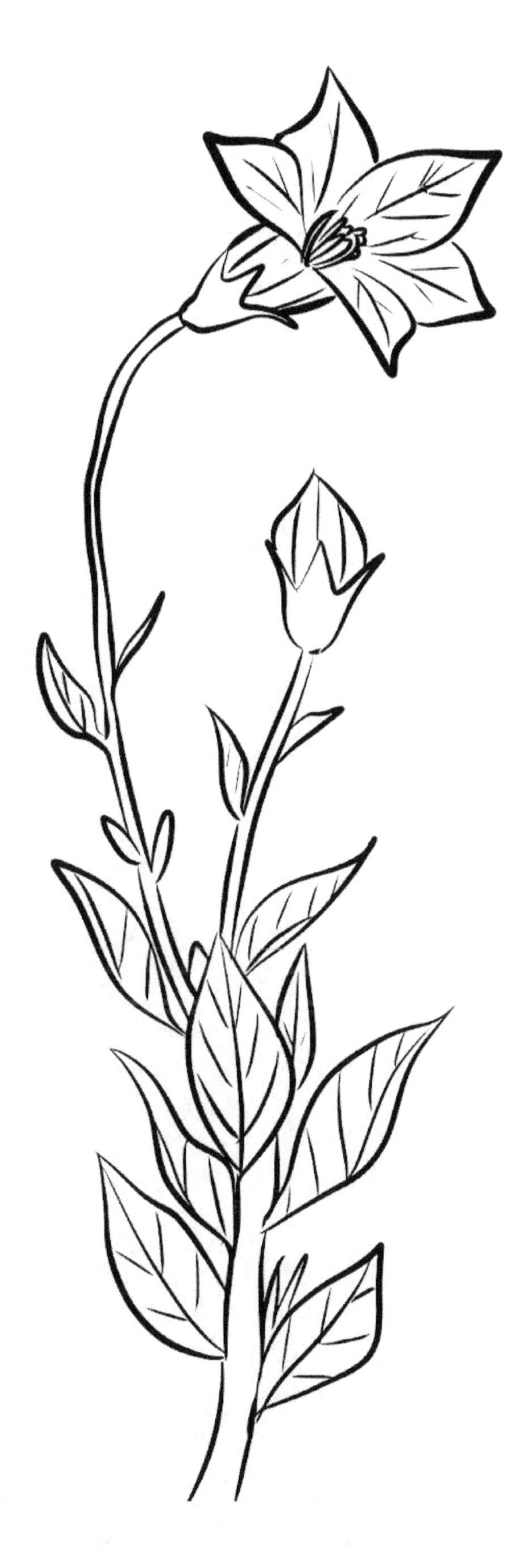

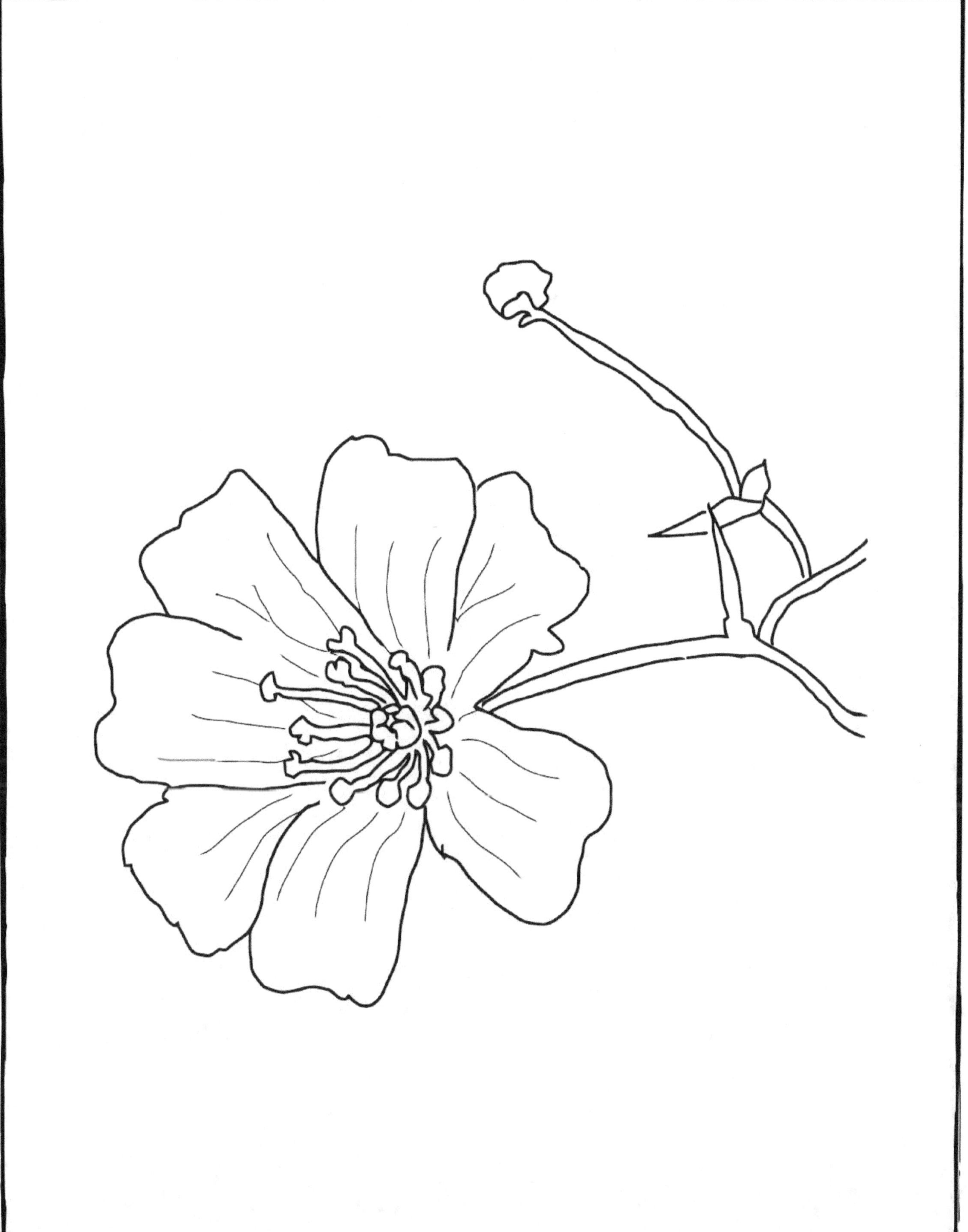

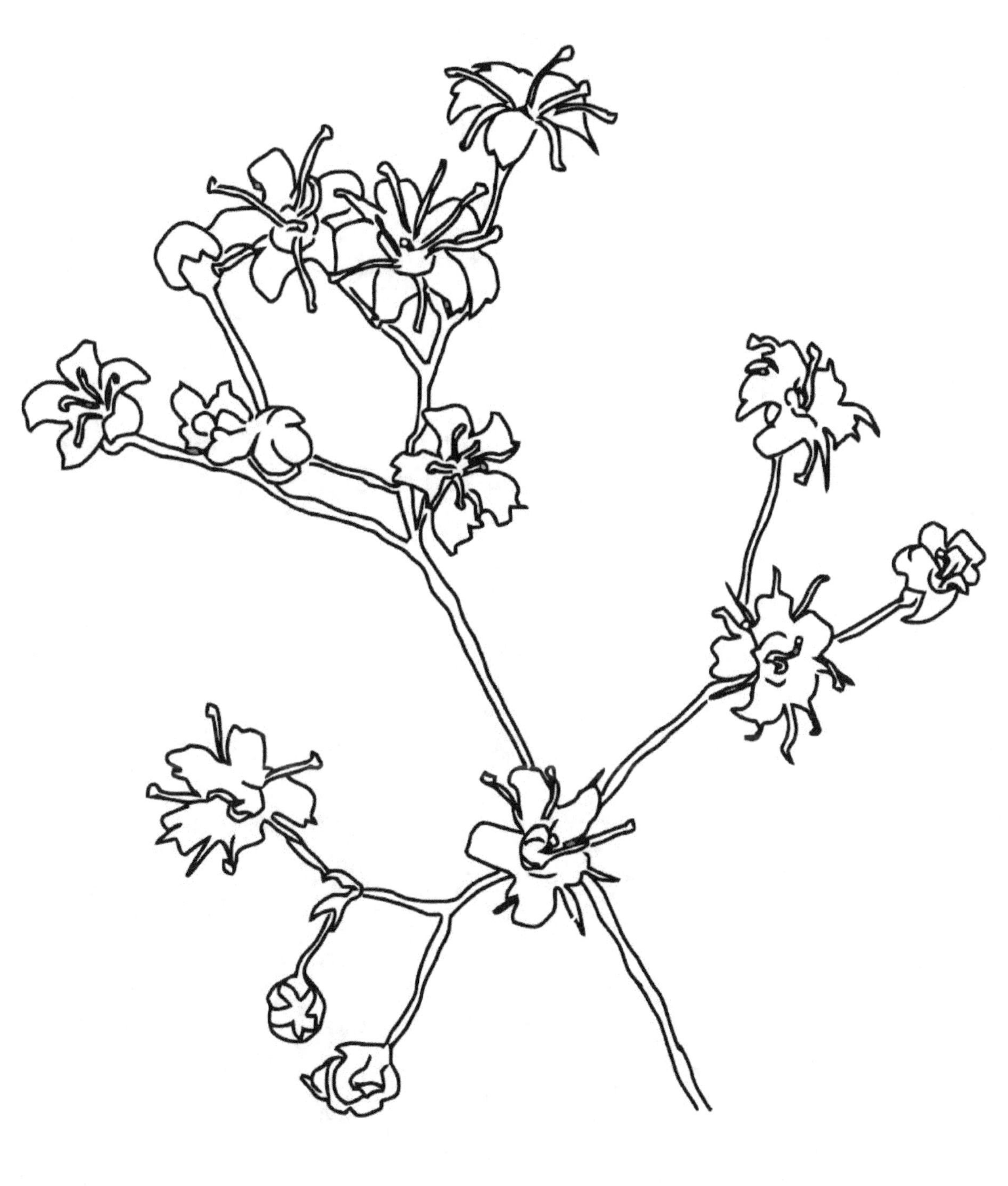

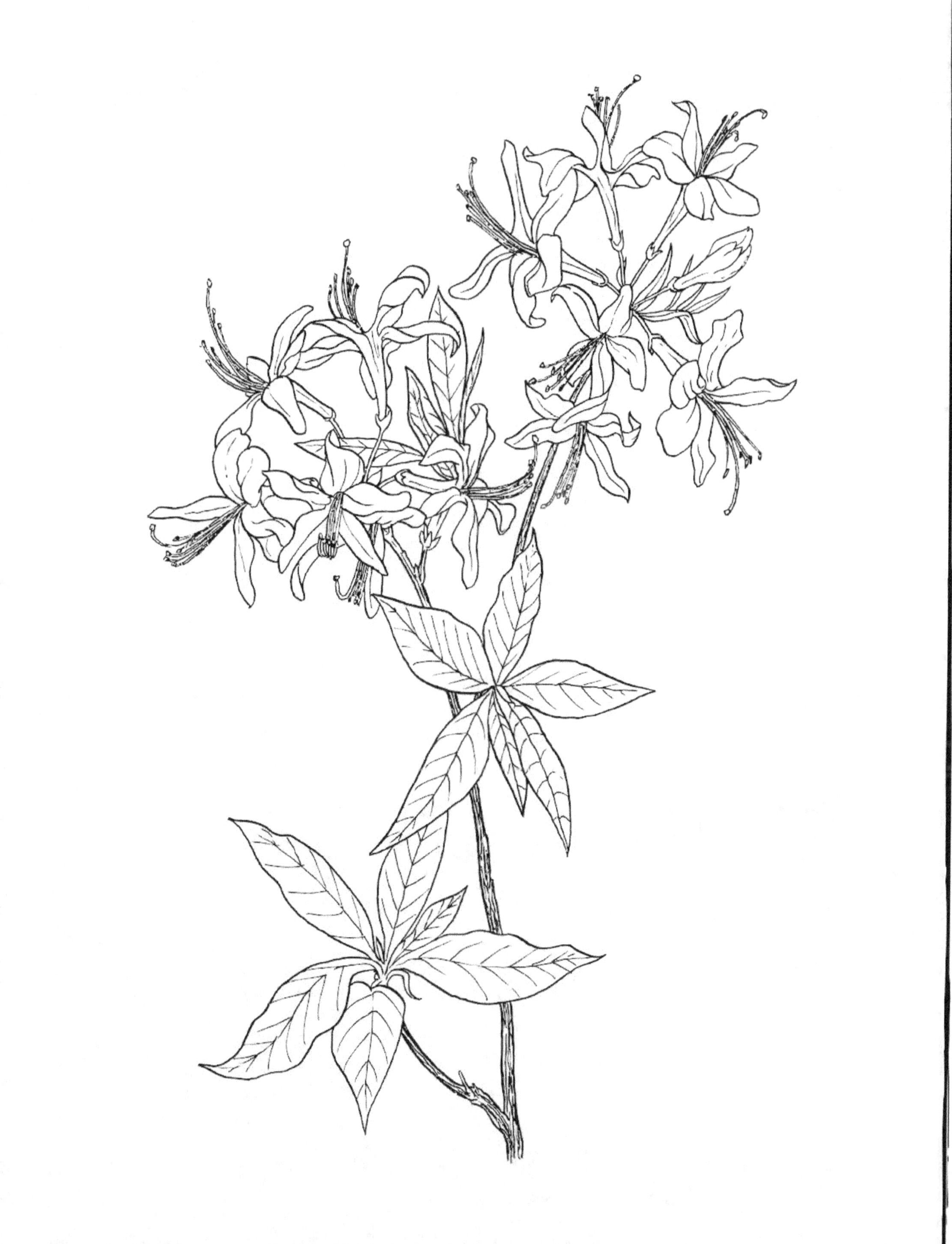

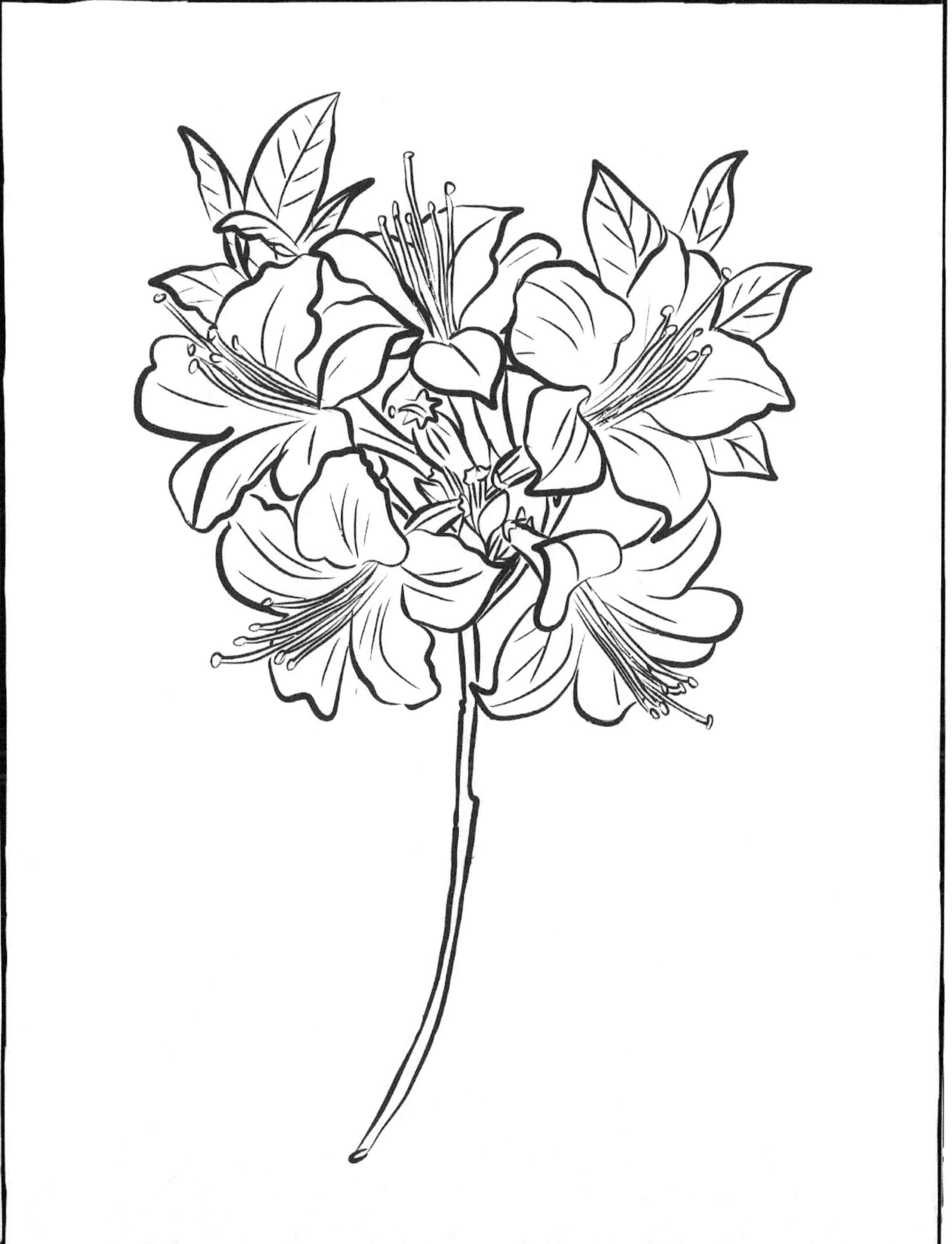